VOCABULARY
WORKSHOP

LEVEL GREEN

Sadlier-Oxford
A Division of William H. Sadlier, Inc.
New York, NY 10005-1002

VOCABULARY WORKSHOP

Reviewers

Lynn Chapman
Third Grade Teacher
Tomball, TX

Sharon West
Third Grade Teacher
Tallahassee, FL

Deborah A. Burns
Third Grade Teacher
Hillsborough, NJ

Kim Cornish
Third Grade Teacher
Tallahassee, FL

Diane Flora
Reading Specialist
Indianapolis, IN

Sr. M. Francis Regis Trojano, CSJ
Educational Consultant
Boston, MA

Acknowledgments

Archive Photos: 125.

Corbis/ Kevin R. Morris: 19; Kevin Fleming: 25; Roger Wood: 31; Layne Kennedy: 61; Pallava Bagla: 77; Wally McNamee: 83; Josef Scaylea: 89; Corbis: 95, 107; Bettmann: 113.

The Image Works/ David Lassman: 55; Suzanne Dunn: 119.

Stone/ Jean-Marc Truchet: 43; John Kelly: 49.

FPG/ Vcg: 13.

Illustrator

Daryl Stevens: 16, 22, 28, 34, 41, 46, 52, 58, 64, 71, 80, 86, 92, 98, 105, 110, 116, 122, 128, 135

CONTENTS

FOREWORD

For nearly half a century Vocabulary Workshop has proven a highly successful tool for promoting and guiding systematic vocabulary growth. Level Green is meant both to help younger students *increase* their vocabulary and to *improve* their vocabulary skills. It has also been designed to help prepare students for vocabulary-related items found in standardized tests.

Mastery of the words introduced in this text will make students better readers and better writers—better readers because they will be able to understand and appreciate more of what they read, and better writers because they will have at hand a greater pool of words with which to express themselves. Many of the words introduced in this book are ones that students will encounter in social studies, science, and literature, as well as in their reading outside the classroom.

Word List   Level Green contains 160 basic words selected on the basis of currency in present-day usage, frequency in recognized vocabulary lists and on standardized tests, and the latest grade-placement research.

Units   The words are grouped in 16 short, stimulating units that include: definitions (with pronunciation and parts of speech), reinforcement of meanings, synonyms and antonyms, in-context sentence completions, and word-association exercises.

Reviews   Four Reviews (one for every four units) reinforce the work of the units with challenging exercises that include Spelling, Vocabulary in Context, Analogies, Word Families, and Word Games.

Two Cumulative Reviews, the first covering the first 8 units and the second covering the last 8 units, provide further reinforcement.

Assessment   The Diagnostic Test provides ready assessment of student needs and preparedness at the outset of the term.

The Final Mastery Test provides end-of-term assessment of student achievement.

Teacher Materials   A Teacher's Annotated Edition supplies answers to all of the exercises in the pupil text and an introduction to the Vocabulary Workshop program.

The Supplementary Testing Program provides separate testing exercises covering the material found in the pupil text. Answers are in the Teacher's Annotated Edition.

NOTE TO STUDENTS

Most of the vocabulary words in this book will be new to you. Some you may recognize, though you may not be sure of what they mean. Others you may not know at all. The 160 unit words introduced in this book have been chosen because they are useful words to know. You will see them in school books, on tests, and in the books and magazines you read at home. You will hear these words spoken by teachers, by television reporters, by people in government, and by people in business. By the time you finish this book, you will have learned not only the meanings of these words but also how and when they are used. They will become part of your personal vocabulary. They will help you to become a better reader, a better writer, and a better speaker, too.

In the Definition sections of this book, you will be given the pronunciations, the parts of speech, and the meanings of these words. You will also be given examples of how they are used in sentences, as well as some of their synonyms and antonyms. Here and on the next four pages you will learn more about these and other vocabulary terms.

PRONUNCIATION KEY

The pronunciation of a word is the way it is spoken. In this book, the pronunciation of each unit word appears directly below it in the Definitions section.

The pronunciation shows how the word should be spoken and how it is broken into syllables. To find how to speak a unit word, compare the symbols given in the pronunciation with the key printed below. The symbols are similar to those used in most standard dictionaries. The accent mark (') shows the syllable in the word that should be stressed, or spoken with more force. In this book the accent mark comes before the syllable that should be stressed. In some dictionaries the mark comes after.

Vowels	ā	lake	e	let	ü	boot, new
	a	mat	ī	knife	u̇	foot, pull
	â	care	i	sit	ə	rug, broken
	ä	bark, bottle	ō	flow	ər	bird, better
	au̇	doubt	ô	all, cord		
	ē	beat, wordy	oi	oil		

Consonants	ch	child, lecture	s	cellar	wh	what
	g	give	sh	shoe	y	yell
	j	gentle, bridge	th	thank	z	is
	ŋ	sing	ŧh	those	zh	measure

All other consonants are sounded as in the alphabet.

Stress	The accent mark *precedes* the syllable receiving the major stress: en 'rich

THE VOCABULARY OF VOCABULARY

English has a large group of special terms to describe how words are used and how they are related to one another. These terms make up what we might call the "vocabulary of vocabulary." Learning to understand and use the "vocabulary of vocabulary" will help you to get better results in your vocabulary-building program.

Part of Speech

Every word in English plays some role in the language. What that role is determines how a word is classified grammatically. These classifications are called "parts of speech." In English there are eight parts of speech: nouns, pronouns, verbs, adjectives, adverbs, prepositions, conjunctions, and interjections. All of the words introduced in this book are nouns (abbreviated *n.*), verbs (*v.*), or adjectives (*adj.*).

A **noun** names a person, place, or thing. *Brother, city*, and *pencil* are nouns. So are *Columbus, Dallas*, and *Congress*. Nouns also name things such as ideas and feelings; for example, *freedom* and *joy* are nouns.

Verbs express action or a state of being. *Do, find, say, lose, remember, skip, laugh, dig,* and *pretend* are verbs.

Adjectives describe or give information about nouns or other adjectives. *Big, little, near, far, blue, bright, ugly, helpful,* and *mean* are adjectives.

Many English words act as more than one part of speech. The word *fan*, for example, can be a verb or a noun. Its part of speech depends upon the way it is used.

NOUN: We bought a *fan* for the kitchen last week. [*fan* names a thing]

VERB: I need to *fan* myself to stay cool. [*fan* expresses an action]

EXERCISES   Circle the choice that identifies the part of speech of the word in **dark print.**

1. It was a **good** vacation.
     a. noun   b. verb   c. adjective

2. Let's **swim** to the other end of the pool.
     a. noun   b. verb   c. adjective

3. I had a good **swim** yesterday.
     a. noun   b. verb   c. adjective

4. That was a **beautiful** song.
     a. noun   b. verb   c. adjective

5. He is in such a deep **sleep.**
     a. noun   b. verb   c. adjective

6. I need to **sleep** at least nine hours a night.
     a. noun   b. verb   c. adjective

Synonyms and Antonyms

Synonyms

A **synonym** is a word that means *the same* or *nearly the same* as another word.

EXAMPLES big — large   joy — happiness

yell — shout   start — begin

anger — rage   author – writer

EXERCISES For each of the following groups circle the choice that is most nearly the **same** in meaning as the word in **dark print.**

1. **diary**	2. **choose**	3. **dish**	4. **happy**
a. milk	a. ask	a. sponge	a. cheery
b. sand	b. select	b. knife	b. sad
c. pencil	c. tell	c. table	c. sleepy
d. journal	d. rest	d. plate	d. quiet

Antonyms

An **antonym** is a word that is *opposite* or *nearly opposite* in meaning to another word.

EXAMPLES up — down   give — take

light — dark   buy — sell

short — long   smile — frown

EXERCISES For each of the following groups circle the choice that is most nearly **opposite** in meaning to the word in **dark print.**

1. **open**	2. **forget**	3. **clean**	4. **start**
a. watch	a. pack	a. dirty	a. begin
b. close	b. travel	b. sad	b. continue
c. drink	c. dance	c. happy	c. stop
d. eat	d. remember	d. pretty	d. wait

Context Clues

When you turn to the "Completing the Sentence" and "Vocabulary in Context" exercises in this book, look for clues built into the passages to guide you to the correct answers. There are three basic types of clues.

Restatement Clues   A restatement clue gives a *definition of*, or a *synonym for*, a missing word.

EXAMPLE   The <u>cheerful</u> mood during the holidays made me feel
_____ too.

a. tired   b. hungry   c. sad   (d.) happy

Contrast Clues   A contrast clue gives an *antonym for*, or a phrase meaning *the opposite of*, a missing word.

EXAMPLE   Because we did not have time to <u>clean</u>, the house remained
_____.

(a.) dirty   b. sunny   c. clean   d. quiet

Situational Clues   Sometimes the situation itself, as it is outlined in the sentence or passage, suggests the word that is missing but does not state the meaning directly.

EXAMPLE   If you don't want to get <u>lost</u> on your next trip, you will have to use a
_____.

a. car   b. train   (c.) map   d. horn

To figure out which word is missing from the sentence, ask yourself this question: What would you have to use so that you don't get lost? a car? a train? a map? a horn?

EXERCISES   Use context clues to choose the word that best completes each of the following sentences.

1. If you're sick and you think you have fever, it's a good idea to take your
_____.

   a. bed   b. bicycle   c. homework   (d.) temperature

2. To clean up a spill, it is best to use a _____.
   a. notebook   (b.) sponge   c. compass   d. pin

3. If you don't like being nervous, then try to stay _____!
   (a.) calm   b. scared   c. hungry   d. dizzy

Analogies

An **analogy** is a comparison. For example, we can make an analogy, or comparison, between a camera and a human eye.

In this book and in many standardized tests, you will be asked to find the relationship between two words. Then, to show that you understand that relationship, you will be asked to choose another pair of words that show the same relationship.

EXAMPLES

1. **whisper** is to **shout** as

   a. ask is to question

   b. sleep is to doze

   c. stay is to go

   d. eat is to swallow

2. **small** is to **little** as

   a. black is to white

   b. happy is to pleased

   c. red is to green

   d. unhappy is to sad

In the first example, note that *whisper* and *shout* are **antonyms;** they are opposite in meaning. Of the four choices given, which pair is made up of words that are also antonyms, or opposite in meaning? The answer, of course, is *c, stay is to go.*

In the second example, note that *small* and *little* are **synonyms;** they have nearly the same meaning. Of the four choices given, which pair is made up of words that are also synonyms, or have nearly the same meaning? The answer is *b, happy is to pleased.*

There are many other kinds of analogies besides ones based on synonyms and antonyms. For each of the exercises that follow, first study carefully the pair of words in **dark print.** Then, when you have figured out the relationship between the two words, look for another pair that has the same relationship. Circle the item that best completes the analogy, and then write the relationship on the lines provided.

3. **brush** is to **paint** as

   a. ruler is to wood

   b. paper is to book

   c. scissors is to cut

   d. eraser is to rubber

4. **finger** is to **hand** as

   a. ear is to sound

   b. leg is to bone

   c. elbow is to knee

   d. toe is to foot

5. **robin** is to **bird** as

   a. cow is to barn

   b. tuna is to fish

   c. dog is to cat

   d. horse is to cart

Relationship: _____

_____

_____

_____

Relationship: _____

_____

_____

_____

Relationship: _____

_____

_____

_____

 **Diagnostic Test** *Circle the letter for the word or phrase that best expresses the meaning of the word in **dark print** in the introductory phrase.*

Example

tore my shirt

a. bought   (b.) ripped   c. washed   d. sold

---

1. **loyal** to our country
   a. new   b. false   c. faithful   d. open

2. as we **wander** through the maze
   a. roam   b. race   c. hop   d. crawl

3. to **capture** a firefly
   a. chase   b. free   c. lose   d. catch

4. **insist** that we stay for dinner
   a. ask   b. demand   c. refuse   d. pray

5. **glance** at the calendar
   a. peek   b. point   c. stare   d. aim

6. such a **precious** gift
   a. dull   b. worthless   c. shiny   d. valuable

7. with us on the **journey**
   a. vote   b. raft   c. trip   d. porch

8. just across the **border**
   a. sea   b. middle   c. boundary   d. street

9. to **imitate** the great artist
   a. question   b. respect   c. blame   d. copy

10. our **custom** after supper

    a. drink   b. habit   c. chore   d. wish

11. inviting her **bashful** cousin

    a. shy   b. older   c. smart   d. famous

12. in a **fury** over our choice

    a. speech   b. dream   c. rage   d. contest

13. was **prompt** for the meeting

    a. late   b. missing   c. in town   d. on time

14. had a strange **origin**

    a. ending   b. beginning   c. accent   d. plan

15. suffered a **grave** injury

    a. small   b. head   c. serious   d. surprising

16. might **kindle** your interest

    a. stir up   b. notice   c. match   d. dull

17. a **wretched** case of the flu

    a. mild   b. miserable   c. strange   d. new

18. a solid **barrier**

    a. wall   b. excuse   c. case   d. meal

19. **inspect** the document

    a. write   b. discuss   c. destroy   d. examine

20. a **ripple** of applause

    a. sound   b. round   c. wave   d. crash

Definitions *Study the spelling, pronunciation, part of speech, and definition for each word. Write the word on the line in the sentence. Then read the synonyms and antonyms.*

1. active
('ak tiv)

(adj.) taking action; full of movement

To be healthy, it is important to stay _____.

SYNONYMS: lively, busy, energetic
ANTONYMS: slow, lazy, passive

2. bargain
('bar gən)

(n.) an agreement between two people or groups; something sold cheaply; a good deal

The baseball cards were a _____ *at $1 a pack.*

(v.) to ask for a lower price; to agree to sell something for less

Not many store owners like to _____ *with customers.*

SYNONYMS: (n.) "steal"; (v.) haggle

3. gasp
(gasp)

(v.) to breathe in quickly or have trouble breathing because of fear or shock; to catch one's breath

I'm sure you're going to _____ *when you see the scary part of the movie.*

(n.) the act of gasping or panting

We heard the sound of a _____ *as the runner crossed the finish line.*

SYNONYM: (v.) pant
ANTONYM: (v.) sigh

4. loyal
('loi əl)

(adj.) faithful to one's country, a person, or an idea

The _____ *soldier was proud to serve his country.*

ANTONYMS: unfaithful, treacherous

5. resource
('re sôrs)

(n.) a source of useful supplies, materials, or information

An encyclopedia is a valuable _____.

SYNONYM: supply

A father playfully **struggles** (word 7) in a game of tug-of-war with his three young children.

6. **sensitive** ('sen sə tiv)

(adj.) reacting to something quickly; easily hurt or bothered

My teeth are _____ *to cold drinks.*

SYNONYMS: touchy, responsive, delicate
ANTONYMS: insensitive, uncaring

7. **struggle** ('strə gəl)

(n.) an enormous effort or attempt; a battle

It was a _____ *to climb the mountain.*

(v.) to try hard; to make a great effort; to fight

The team had to _____ *to win the ball game.*

SYNONYMS: (n.) effort; (v.) strive, battle, wrestle

8. **value** ('val yü)

(n.) something important; the worth of something; an amount

I did not know the _____ *of the painting.*

(v.) to estimate the worth of; to think highly of

I _____ *your opinion because you are so wise.*

SYNONYMS: (n.) total, sum, quantity, worth, importance;
(v.) assess, estimate, evaluate, price, treasure
ANTONYMS: (v.) belittle, scorn, reject

9. **vary** ('var ē)

(v.) to do in a new way; to make different; to change

To make lunch interesting, _____ *your choice of vegetables.*

SYNONYMS: change, alter

10. **wander** ('wan dər)

(v.) to move around without a plan or goal; to get lost

Did you see the deer _____ *into our backyard?*

SYNONYMS: roam, ramble, meander, stray
ANTONYMS: stay, remain

Choose the word whose meaning is suggested by the clue given. Then write the word on the line provided.

1. To be _____ to your country is to be faithful to it.
   a. active   b. loyal   c. sensitive

2. When you _____ your tasks, you change them.
   a. gasp   b. wander   c. vary

3. A source of useful materials is a _____.
   a. resource   b. bargain   c. value

4. If you _____ off without thinking, you can get lost.
   a. gasp   b. struggle   c. wander

5. To _____ is to take in a deep breath.
   a. bargain   b. gasp   c. vary

6. Soccer is a(n) _____ sport because the players move a lot.
   a. loyal   b. sensitive   c. active

7. The worth of a car will tell you its _____.
   a. struggle   b. resource   c. value

8. _____ people can get their feelings hurt easily.
   a. Sensitive   b. Active   c. Loyal

9. When you _____ for something, you often end up paying a lower price.
   a. vary   b. bargain   c. wander

10. To work at a new and difficult job can be a _____.
    a. struggle   b. value   c. gasp

Synonyms

*Choose the word that is most nearly the **same** in meaning as the word or phrase in **dark print**. Then write your choice on the line provided.*

1. **treasure** their advice
   a. bargain   b. vary   c. value   _____

2. an **effort** to walk
   a. resource   b. value   c. struggle   _____

3. a **supply** of sports equipment
   a. bargain   b. value   c. resource   _____

4. **roam** into the woods
   a. vary   b. bargain   c. wander   _____

5. **change** your direction
   a. vary   b. struggle   c. bargain   _____

6. **haggle** for a better price
   a. gasp   b. wander   c. bargain   _____

Antonyms

*Choose the word that is most nearly the **opposite** in meaning to the word or phrase in **dark print**. Then write your choice on the line provided.*

1. an **unfaithful** citizen
   a. loyal   b. active   c. sensitive   _____

2. a **slow** morning
   a. sensitive   b. active   c. loyal   _____

3. an **uncaring** companion
   a. sensitive   b. loyal   c. active   _____

4. **sigh** deeply
   a. bargain   b. wander   c. gasp   _____

From the list of words on pages 12–13, choose the one that best completes each item below. Then write the word on the line provided. (You may have to change the word's ending.)

Tools

Our neighbor is a carpenter. If you _____ into her garage, you will find many tools.

She knows the _____ of tools. She takes care of them so that they will last a long time.

Our neighbor often buys paint. She is _____ to her favorite brand of paint and won't buy any other kind. She was happy to find out that the price of paint in the new hardware store is a _____. She used to pay much more for the same paint in other stores.

Carpenters have to be physically _____. They move around a lot while they work.

Seasons

In the summer, the weather in the mountains can _____. It might be hot in the morning, rainy in the early afternoon, and cool in the evening.

People with _____ skin can get bad sunburns in the summer if they don't wear suntan lotion.

Autumn is a good time for raking leaves. Leaves are a _____ of minerals for the soil.

It can be a _____ getting to school when there is a snowstorm. It's hard to walk or to drive!

Your first breath of the icy air can make you _____!

*Circle the letter next to the choice that best completes the sentence or answers the question. Pay special attention to the word in **dark print**.*

1. You **vary** your lunch if you eat
   a. too slowly.
   b. just an apple.
   c. different foods each day.
   d. pizza every day.

2. During a **struggle**, you might expect a person to
   a. fall asleep.
   b. relax.
   c. have a hard time.
   d. have a good time.

3. My very **active** puppy is probably
   a. sleeping.
   b. singing.
   c. breathing.
   d. digging.

4. A toy is a good **value** if it is
   a. not worth anything.
   b. worth a lot.
   c. hard to use.
   d. easy to use.

5. Which is a **resource** for tools?
   a. a bakery
   b. a hammer
   c. a dress shop
   d. a hardware store

6. You cry, "It's a **bargain**!" That means you
   a. give a present.
   b. give something away.
   c. get something more cheaply.
   d. pay too much.

7. Expect a **loyal** friend to
   a. tell your secrets.
   b. stick by you.
   c. desert you.
   d. do nothing for you.

8. Harsh soap makes **sensitive** skin
   a. clean and shiny.
   b. soft and smooth.
   c. sudsy and foamy.
   d. itchy and sore.

9. If your mind **wanders**, you might
   a. lose your place.
   b. get hungry.
   c. think clearly.
   d. get a phone call.

10. You **gasp** when
    a. you read a long story.
    b. your team comes from behind to win the game.
    c. you sit down to eat.
    d. relax in your favorite chair.

Definitions Study the spelling, pronunciation, part of speech, and definition for each word. Write the word on the line in the sentence. Then read the synonyms and antonyms.

1. **capture**
('kap chər)

(n.) the act of catching or gaining control by force or skill

After the _____ of the ship by the pirates, they divided its gold and silver.

(v.) to grab and hold onto; to hold the attention of

I will not read a book that does not _____ my interest.

SYNONYMS: (v.) catch, grab, seize, clutch, grasp
ANTONYMS: (v.) lose, release

2. **coward**
(kaů ərd)

(n.) one who has no courage or gets scared easily

I behaved like a _____ during the thunderstorm.

SYNONYMS: weakling, wimp
ANTONYM: hero

3. **exclaim**
(eks 'klām)

(v.) to speak with strong feelings or emotions; to cry out

Whenever the phone rings, I always _____, "I'll get it!"

SYNONYMS: yell, shout, proclaim
ANTONYMS: whisper, murmur

4. **gloomy**
('glü mē)

(adj.) partly or completely dark; wearing a frown

The twins were both _____ when they did not get their way.

SYNONYMS: unhappy, miserable, sullen
ANTONYMS: bright, happy, cheerful

5. **insist**
(in 'sist)

(v.) to state something or make a demand firmly

I continued to _____ that I did my homework even though I didn't have it with me.

SYNONYMS: declare, maintain, stress, require, persist

A child concentrates while playing a **passage** (word 6) of music.

6. passage
('pa sij)

(n.) the act of moving from one place to another; a trip by sea or by air; a way in or out; a part of a written work or piece of music

The _____ from England to India took a few days by boat.

SYNONYMS: tunnel, passageway, entrance, exit, opening, piece, paragraph, section

7. restless
('rest lis)

(adj.) without rest or sleep; unable to rest, relax, or be still

The baby was _____ all night.

SYNONYMS: nervous, uneasy, impatient
ANTONYMS: relaxed, peaceful, patient

8. shallow
('sha lō)

(adj.) measuring little from bottom to top; not deep; not showing much thought

The lake is _____, so it is safe.

SYNONYMS: empty, simple
ANTONYMS: deep, far

9. shatter
('sha tər)

(v.) to break into many pieces; to cause much damage

Why did the mirror _____?

SYNONYMS: smash, demolish, ruin

10. talent
('tal ənt)

(n.) an ability to do something well; a skill or gift

You have a natural _____ for singing.

SYNONYMS: gift, skill, knack

Match the Meaning

Choose the word whose meaning is suggested by the clue given. Then write the word on the line provided.

1. Someone who _____ speaks in an excited way.
   a. captures   b. shatters   c. exclaims

2. A _____ sink does not go down too far.
   a. shallow   b. restless   c. gloomy

3. To _____ an object is to grab and hold on to it.
   a. exclaim   b. insist   c. capture

4. A _____ is a person who is afraid or fearful.
   a. talent   b. passage   c. coward

5. A tunnel is a _____ that goes from one end to the other.
   a. passage   b. capture   c. talent

6. If you have a skill, you have a _____.
   a. coward   b. talent   c. passage

7. When you can't sit still, you are _____.
   a. shallow   b. gloomy   c. restless

8. When a glass falls to the floor, it will probably _____.
   a. insist   b. capture   c. shatter

9. A clown can make both happy and _____ faces.
   a. restless   b. gloomy   c. shallow

10. When I _____ on something, I do not give up.
    a. capture   b. insist   c. exclaim

*Choose the word that is most nearly the **same** in meaning as the word or phrase in **dark print.** Then write your choice on the line provided.*

1. a **skill** for baking
   a. passage   b. coward   c. talent   _____

2. an **entrance** to the school
   a. capture   b. passage   c. coward   _____

3. **maintain** their rights
   a. capture   b. shatter   c. insist on   _____

4. **break** into a hundred pieces
   a. capture   b. insist   c. shatter   _____

5. **uneasy** with worry
   a. gloomy   b. restless   c. shallow   _____

Antonyms

*Choose the word that is most nearly the **opposite** in meaning to the word or phrase in **dark print.** Then write your choice on the line provided.*

1. painted in **cheerful** colors
   a. gloomy   b. shallow   c. restless   _____

2. **lose** the chess piece
   a. insist on   b. capture   c. shatter   _____

3. **whisper** your answer
   a. capture   b. insist   c. exclaim   _____

4. played a **hero** on stage
   a. talent   b. passage   c. coward   _____

5. a **deep** swimming pool
   a. restless   b. gloomy   c. shallow   _____

Completing the Sentence

From the list of words on pages 18–19, choose the one that best completes each item below. Then write the word on the line provided. (You may have to change the word's ending.)

Games

I like to play games with my brothers and sisters. We enjoy swimming in the neighborhood pool. We always stay in the _____ end to make sure that we are safe.

We play baseball in our backyard. We know that if we hit the ball too hard, it might hit the house and _____ a window. Then the people in the house would _____, "Hey, you broke my window!"

Jumping rope is fun. I _____ on being the first one to start jumping rope! That is because I get very _____ when I have to wait.

When I'm feeling _____, playing games can put me in a much better mood!

The Underground Railroad

In the years before the Civil War, many brave men and women risked their lives to free the slaves. It was very dangerous work and not a job for a _____.

One way that slaves escaped to freedom was by using a _____ known as "The Underground Railroad."

Harriet Tubman showed a _____ for not getting caught by going back and forth on "The Underground Railroad" and helping many slaves escape.

It was wonderful how many slaves escaped and managed to avoid _____.

*Circle the letter next to the choice that best completes the sentence or answers the question. Pay special attention to the word in **dark print.***

1. To **shatter** a vase is to
   a. break it into pieces.
   b. put flowers in it.
   c. wash it carefully.
   d. replace it.

2. **Shallow** water comes up to my
   a. shoulders.
   b. ears.
   c. ankles.
   d. waist.

3. If you read a **passage** of a story, you
   a. read the whole story.
   b. read a part of the story.
   c. read none of the story.
   d. understand the whole story.

4. It is best to **capture** a moth
   a. with a fan.
   b. with a hook.
   c. with a net.
   d. with a pet.

5. Which shows that you **insist**?
   a. "May I come in?"
   b. "Will you join me?"
   c. "It has to be my way."
   d. "Whatever you think is okay."

6. A **coward** gets easily
   a. cold.
   b. scared.
   c. bored.
   d. thirsty.

7. Someone with **talent** might
   a. win a prize.
   b. go to sleep.
   c. go to the doctor.
   d. come in last.

8. Which words might you **exclaim**?
   a. "Where is the nearest store?"
   b. "My dog ran away!"
   c. "What kind of soup is that?"
   d. "What day is it?"

9. A person who is **gloomy** doesn't
   a. frown.
   b. swim.
   c. wink.
   d. smile.

10. When I'm **restless**, I can't
    a. remember the words.
    b. keep still.
    c. stop yawning.
    d. get warm.

Definitions *Study the spelling, pronunciation, part of speech, and definition for each word. Write the word on the line in the sentence. Then read the synonyms and antonyms.*

1. **atmosphere**
('at mə sfir)

(n.) the air that surrounds the earth; the feeling or mood in a room or place

The earth's _____ is made up of invisible gases.

SYNONYMS: mood, environment

2. **brilliant**
('bril yənt)

(adj.) sparkling or full of light; striking and shiny; very smart

Many stars in the universe are _____.

SYNONYMS: bright, shining, sparkling, intense, vivid, outstanding, remarkable, smart, clever
ANTONYMS: dull, lifeless

3. **convince**
('kən vins)

(v.) to get someone to believe something or to do something; to win over

It is easy to _____ me to eat two pieces of carrot cake.

SYNONYMS: persuade, urge, coax
ANTONYM: dissuade

4. **endure**
(in 'dúr)

(v.) to put up with; to continue in the same way for a long time

I cannot _____ your silly jokes!

SYNONYMS: suffer, bear, withstand, last

5. **glance**
(glans)

(v.) to look quickly; to bounce off a surface and fly off to one side

I will _____ at my watch from time to time to make sure my speech isn't too long.

(n.) a quick look

I took one _____ at you, and I knew we would be close friends.

SYNONYMS: (v. & n.) look, glimpse, peek
ANTONYM: (v. & n.) stare

People looking for fun and thrills take the **plunge** (word 7) in a roller coaster.

6. harsh
(harsh)

(adj.) rough or unpleasant to the senses; unkind in voice or behavior

Try not to speak in a _____ tone, even when you are angry.

SYNONYMS: crude, unpleasant, cruel, severe, demanding, rough
ANTONYMS: smooth, pleasant, kind

7. plunge
(plənj)

(v.) to fall quickly; to quickly throw oneself down or into something

They say the temperature will _____ tomorrow, so wear a warm coat!

(n.) the act of jumping in

Enjoy taking a _____ into the pool!

SYNONYMS: (v.) fall, dive, drop; (n.) dive, swim

8. precious
('pre shəs)

(adj.) sells for a very high price; loved and adored

Sapphires and rubies are _____ jewels.

SYNONYMS: valuable, special
ANTONYMS: worthless, valueless, ordinary

9. swift
(swift)

(adj.) able to move at quick speed; quick to respond

A speed skater's arm and leg movements are _____.

SYNONYMS: fast, rapid, speedy, ready
ANTONYMS: slow, gradual

10. unite
(yü 'nīt)

(v.) to bring two or more parts together to make a whole

The team's players need to _____ during a game.

SYNONYMS: join, combine
ANTONYMS: break, split, undo, divide

25

Match the Meaning

Choose the word whose meaning is suggested by the clue given. Then write the word on the line provided.

1. A very bright moon might be described as _____.
   a. brilliant   b. swift   c. harsh

2. To _____ something is to suffer through it.
   a. convince   b. plunge   c. endure

3. Sandpaper can feel _____ against your skin.
   a. harsh   b. brilliant   c. precious

4. A toy that is loved and adored is said to be _____.
   a. harsh   b. swift   c. precious

5. To _____ all the parts is to make a whole of them.
   a. convince   b. unite   c. endure

6. As soon as you walk into a room, you can feel its _____.
   a. atmosphere   b. glance   c. plunge

7. A person who is able to respond quickly might be described as _____.
   a. precious   b. harsh   c. swift

8. To _____ into a task is to jump into it and get it done.
   a. convince   b. endure   c. plunge

9. If you _____ at something, you give it a quick look.
   a. glance   b. convince   c. plunge

10. It is not always easy to _____ people to do something difficult.
    a. endure   b. plunge   c. convince

Synonyms

*Choose the word that is most nearly the **same** in meaning as the word or phrase in **dark print**. Then write your choice on the line provided.*

1. **dive** into the sea
   a. unite   b. convince   c. plunge   _____

2. a winter coat that will **last**
   a. endure   b. glance   c. unite   _____

3. **coax** me to take dance lessons
   a. convince   b. endure   c. unite   _____

4. a smelly **environment**
   a. plunge   b. glance   c. atmosphere   _____

5. **glimpse** at the newspaper
   a. glance   b. convince   c. unite   _____

6. a **valuable** gift
   a. harsh   b. precious   c. swift   _____

Antonyms

*Choose the word that is most nearly the **opposite** in meaning to the word or phrase in **dark print**. Then write your choice on the line provided.*

1. **divide** the group
   a. endure   b. convince   c. unite   _____

2. a **lifeless** performance
   a. brilliant   b. swift   c. harsh   _____

3. a **gradual** movement
   a. brilliant   b. harsh   c. swift   _____

4. a **kind** comment
   a. harsh   b. precious   c. swift   _____

From the list of words on pages 24–25, choose the one that best completes each item below. Then write the word on the line provided. (You may have to change the word's ending.)

Vacation

Every summer, my sister and I _____ on a vacation idea and together try to make our parents believe that it's a good one.

This year, we hoped to _____ our parents to take the family to a theme park in Florida.

We like the fun _____ in Florida. Everyone always seems to be having such a good time!

Also, after such a cold and _____ winter, we thought it would be nice to go someplace warm.

My parents do not agree. They think it is too hot in Florida. It is hard for them to _____ the heat.

I know that wherever we go on vacation, we'll have many _____ memories!

Math

Math can be fun. The best way to do a hard math problem is to _____ right into it.

My math teacher likes us to try to solve problems in our heads, using mental math. He sometimes asks us to add two columns of numbers by taking a quick look at them. Unfortunately, not many of us can solve problems at a _____.

Mental math is a _____ way to solve simple math problems. But sometimes, the fast way is not the best way. Using paper and pencil is sometimes easier.

In our class, there are some _____ math students. They are so smart and get almost every answer correct!

*Circle the letter next to the choice that best completes the sentence or answers the question. Pay special attention to the word in **dark print**.*

1. After a **brilliant** play, fans might
   a. yawn.
   b. boo.
   c. cheer.
   d. leave.

2. To **glance** at a magazine is to
   a. look at it slowly.
   b. look at it quickly.
   c. look at it carefully.
   d. throw it away.

3. Which animal is the most **swift**?
   a. deer
   b. snail
   c. turtle
   d. cow

4. Which is most likely to **endure**?
   a. paper
   b. brick
   c. fruit
   d. flowers

5. A **precious** gift is one that I will
   a. return for another.
   b. give to my dog.
   c. hope never to get.
   d. value forever.

6. Which are **harsh** words?
   a. "We love you."
   b. "You are clever."
   c. "I hate you."
   d. "This cheers me up."

7. The earth's **atmosphere** includes
   a. people and houses.
   b. animals and plants.
   c. oceans and mountains.
   d. air and gases.

8. You're most likely to **plunge**
   a. into an ocean.
   b. into a chair.
   c. into a basement.
   d. into a cake mix.

9. Students would **unite** to sing
   a. off-key.
   b. softly.
   c. together.
   d. apart.

10. You need to **convince** me if you know that I
    a. already like your idea.
    b. do not agree with you.
    c. believe in you.
    d. will do whatever you say

Definitions — *Study the spelling, pronunciation, part of speech, and definition for each word. Write the word on the line in the sentence. Then read the synonyms and antonyms.*

1. **border**
   ('bor dər)

   (n.) the outer edge of an object; the line where one part ends and another starts

   We crossed the _____ into Canada.

   (v.) to be next to or near something; to touch at the edge

   One city can _____ a number of small towns.

   SYNONYMS: (n.) edge, boundary; (v.) bound

2. **certain**
   ('sər tən)

   (adj.) having no doubt; sure; known but not named

   I am _____ I locked the door.

   SYNONYMS: positive, confident, definite, fixed, settled, agreed
   ANTONYMS: uncertain, unsure, indefinite

3. **clasp**
   (klasp)

   (n.) a device that holds parts together; a strong hold

   I lost the _____ to my watch.

   (v.) to hook something up; to hold onto tightly

   My younger sister likes to _____ my hand.

   SYNONYMS: (n.) hook, bar, buckle, grasp; (v.) fasten, attach, buckle, grasp, seize
   ANTONYMS: (v.) undo, loosen, detach, unfasten

4. **depart**
   (di 'pärt)

   (v.) to go away

   Let us know when you _____ for New York.

   SYNONYM: leave
   ANTONYMS: stay, remain

5. **fierce**
   (fērs)

   (adj.) violent; wild or savage; very strong

   The tiger that attacked the zookeeper was _____.

   SYNONYMS: cruel, intense, ferocious
   ANTONYMS: mild, easygoing, placid

Among the **treasures** (word 9) found in King Tutankhamun's tomb were a gold coffin, assorted rings, bracelets, earrings, amulets, and even 415 statues of servants who would do chores for King Tut in the afterlife!

6. **journey**
('jər nē)

(n.) a long trip; a passage from one place to another

Where did you go on your _____?

(v.) to go on a trip; to travel

Enjoy your _____ to Egypt!

SYNONYMS: (n.) trip, expedition, tour, voyage, outing; (v.) tour, travel, trek, go

7. **observe**
(əb 'zərv)

(v.) to see; to watch with close attention; to stick to or obey

I watched you _____ the bird's movements.

SYNONYMS: notice, abide, comply, obey

8. **superb**
(sü 'pərb)

(adj.) of the best quality

The acting and singing in the concert was _____.

SYNONYMS: excellent, splendid, wonderful, marvelous, magnificent
ANTONYMS: inferior, ordinary

9. **treasure**
('tre zhər)

(n.) a collection of valuable objects; something worth a lot

In fairy tales, queens might have soldiers guarding their _____.

(v.) to care a great deal for

I _____ my collection of foreign coins.

SYNONYMS: (n.) wealth, riches; (v.) cherish, prize, appreciate
ANTONYMS: (v.) neglect, disregard

10. **wisdom**
('wiz dəm)

(n.) knowledge and good sense, especially as a result of experience

Grandparents have much _____ about life.

SYNONYMS: judgment, understanding, intelligence, knowledge
ANTONYM: ignorance

 **Choose the word whose meaning is suggested by the clue given. Then write the word on the line provided.**

1. To cherish your friends is to _____ them.
   a. border   b. clasp   c. treasure

2. If you are sure about something, you are _____.
   a. superb   b. certain   c. fierce

3. The edge of something is also called its _____.
   a. border   b. journey   c. wisdom

4. To _____ from your route is to change it.
   a. clasp   b. treasure   c. depart

5. A knowing person is said to have _____.
   a. treasure   b. wisdom   c. journey

6. Something excellent might be described as _____.
   a. certain   b. fierce   c. superb

7. To _____ is to go on a trip.
   a. journey   b. clasp   c. treasure

8. A latch is also called a _____.
   a. border   b. wisdom   c. clasp

9. A nurse will _____ patients to see how they feel.
   a. observe   b. treasure   c. depart

10. Some wild animals are _____.
    a. certain   b. superb   c. fierce

Synonyms

*Choose the word that is most nearly the **same** in meaning as the word or phrase in **dark print**. Then write your choice on the line provided.*

1. **notice** her face
   a. observe b. border c. journey _____

2. **buckle** your seat belts
   a. depart b. clasp c. treasure _____

3. **travel** wherever you want
   a. border b. journey c. treasure _____

4. gain more **knowledge**
   a. clasp b. treasure c. wisdom _____

5. step over the **edge**
   a. journey b. clasp c. border _____

6. a **definite** opinion
   a. fierce b. certain c. superb _____

Antonyms

*Choose the word that is most nearly the **opposite** in meaning to the word or phrase in **dark print**. Then write your choice on the line provided.*

1. **disregard** his ideas
   a. treasure b. border c. clasp _____

2. an **ordinary** meal
   a. fierce b. certain c. superb _____

3. chose to **stay**
   a. border b. treasure c. depart _____

4. an **easygoing** manner
   a. fierce b. superb c. certain _____

Completing the Sentence

From the list of words on pages 30–31, choose the one that best completes each item below. Then write the word on the line provided. (You may have to change the word's ending.)

Traveling to a Foreign Country

When you plan to _____ to a foreign country, it is a good idea to learn how it is different from where you live.

Be sure to _____ all the rules of the country you are visiting. You might get into trouble if you don't obey them!

The rules may change again if you decide to cross over the _____ to visit another country.

Make _____ you know the train schedules.

That way, you will always know when trains arrive and _____.

Soccer

We have a _____ soccer team. Our coach thinks it's the best team she has ever had. We have very good players, and they score many goals each game.

Our coach has a lot of experience. She has much _____ to share with us. She knows that encouraging us to have fun and to get along with each other also helps us to win.

One of our halfbacks forgot to _____ the back of his shin guard, so it fell off during the game.

Soccer games can be very intense. The competition can be _____! Still, we were always ready to take on the other teams. We finished this season on top.

Our team will always _____ the trophy we won.

*Circle the letter next to the choice that best completes the sentence or answers the question. Pay special attention to the word in **dark print**.*

1. Two yards **border** each other if
   a. they have gardens.
   b. they are far apart.
   c. they are side by side.
   d. they are in two different neighborhoods.

2. What do you usually take on a **journey**?
   a. a suitcase
   b. a television set
   c. a mixing bowl
   d. a flag

3. When your teachers agree that you did a **superb** job, it means
   a. they are angry.
   b. they are absent.
   c. they are pleased.
   d. they are upset.

4. If you have **wisdom**, you are
   a. foolish.
   b. sensible.
   c. silly.
   d. afraid.

5. We **depart** from school at around
   a. midnight.
   b. 3:00 P.M.
   c. noon.
   d. 8:30 A.M.

6. If you are **certain,** you can say,
   a. "I don't have a clue."
   b. "Maybe I know."
   c. "I'm not too sure."
   d. "I know for sure."

7. Which animal is the most **fierce**?
   a. lion
   b. rabbit
   c. turtle
   d. lamb

8. Most people **observe** with
   a. forks and knives.
   b. socks and shoes.
   c. eyes and ears.
   d. chins and knees.

9. Which is the smartest place to keep a **treasure**?
   a. in a safe
   b. on a table
   c. under a bed
   d. in a refrigerator

10. If we **clasp** hands, we must be
    a. waving.
    b. clapping.
    c. touching.
    d. smiling.

Selecting Word Meanings

*Circle the choice that is most nearly the **same** in meaning as the word in **dark print**.*

1. had the same **value**
   a. worth   b. scorn   c. battle   d. exit

2. the latest **resource** for writers
   a. job   b. idea   c. information   d. computer

3. the long **passage**
   a. speech   b. tunnel   c. conversation   d. message

4. **journey** to visit my friend
   a. go   b. prepare   c. pack   d. wait

5. to **endure** the noise
   a. encourage   b. combine   c. bear   d. fight

6. got a **harsh** punishment
   a. severe   b. minor   c. gentle   d. fair

7. will **depart** at sunrise
   a. arrive   b. awake   c. leave   d. eat

8. added to my **superb** collection
   a. ordinary   b. excellent   c. first   d. dull

9. always **treasure** this moment
   a. disregard   b. forget   c. appreciate   d. leave

10. **vary** the words in your poem
    a. spell   b. repeat   c. remember   d. change

Spelling *Study the word in **dark print**. If a letter is missing, fill in the blank to make a correctly spelled word. If the word is already spelled correctly, leave the blank empty.*

1. thin **atm__sphere**

2. across the **bo__rder**

3. in a **fier__e** battle

4. found a great **barg__in**

5. led an **a__tive** life

6. the gutless **cow__rd**

7. **exclai__** to the crowd

8. only if you **in__ist**

9. **wi__dom** of the ages

10. **un__ite** for the holiday

Antonyms *Circle the choice that is most nearly the **opposite** in meaning to the word in **dark print**.*

1. the **loyal** soldier
   a. brave   b. healthy   c. faithful   d. unfaithful

2. into this **shallow** bowl
   a. deep   b. empty   c. wooden   d. covered

3. so **restless** a sleeper
   a. peaceful   b. nervous   c. deep   d. uneasy

4. a **precious** book
   a. special   b. worthless   c. long   d. lively

5. **certain** about the time
   a. positive   b. angry   c. unsure   d. worried

Vocabulary in Context

Words have been left out of the following passage. For each item, fill in the circle next to the word in the margin that best fills the blank space.

Elizabeth Cochrane (1867–1922) always wanted to be a writer. She had big ideas and lots of spirit. She hoped to work for a newspaper. But in those days, people thought that only men were tough enough to cover hard news. Elizabeth had to __1__ for a chance. But she would not give up. She changed her name to Nellie Bly. She liked the easy sound of it. Nellie Bly wrote about hard times. Her writing was sharp. Readers loved her.

Nellie Bly had a great deal of __2__. Yet it was hard for women to be on their own a hundred years ago. Nellie Bly had a strong will, however. She moved to New York City. There, she got a job for a big newspaper. She used her special skills to cover unusual stories. As she grew more popular, her ideas grew wilder. Once she pretended to be sick. That way, she could __3__ the bad conditions in a hospital. Another time, she jumped off a ferryboat into a river! She wanted to know how fast rescue workers would come to help her.

Nellie __4__ her boss to send her on a trip around the world. She hoped to beat the record described in a book called *Around the World in Eighty Days*. She traveled by boat, by train, by cart, by camel, and by foot. She sent back stories from the road. Her __5__ was a big success. She broke the fictional record by more than a week. She proved that women could be brave. She also became famous all over the world.

1. ○ gasp
   ○ plunge
   ○ struggle
   ○ wander

2. ○ talent
   ○ pen
   ○ glance
   ○ treasure

3. ○ unite
   ○ support
   ○ destroy
   ○ observe

4. ○ shattered
   ○ convinced
   ○ judged
   ○ shamed

5. ○ atmosphere
   ○ border
   ○ journey
   ○ wisdom

Analogies

Circle the item that best completes the comparison. Then explain the relationship on the lines provided. The first one has been done for you.

1. glance is to **look** as

    a. eye is to ear

    b. loyal is to fierce

    (c.) gasp is to sound

    d. travel is to wander

Relationship: _"Glance" is a type of_

"look;" "gasp" is a type of "sound."

_____

_____

3. capture is to **release** as

    a. sensitive is to gentle

    b. treasure is to ignore

    c. wisdom is to skill

    d. active is to lively

Relationship: _____

_____

_____

2. shatter is to **break** as

    a. talent is to coward

    b. batter is to stake

    c. write is to read

    d. wander is to roam

Relationship: _____

_____

_____

4. clasp is to **necklace** as

    a. buckle is to belt

    b. map is to border

    c. write is to read

    d. bed is to kitchen

Relationship: _____

_____

_____

Challenge: Make up your own

Write a comparison using the words in the box. (Hint: There may be more than one possible answer.) Then explain the relationship on the lines provided.

bargain	fight	struggle	value

Analogy: _____struggle_____ is to _____ as _____ is to _____.

Relationship: _____

Word Families

*The words in **dark print** in the sentences below are related to words introduced in Units 1–4. For example, the nouns* brilliance *and* restlessness *in Item 1 are related to the adjectives* brilliant *(in Unit 3) and* restless *(in Unit 2).*

Circle the related word in **dark print** that best completes each sentence.

atmosphere	depart	glance	precious	swift
brilliant	endure	gloomy	restless	talent
certain	exclaim	loyal	sensitive	unite
coward	fierce	observe	superb	vary

1. You can recognize diamonds by their (**restlessness/brilliance**).

2. The (**cowardly/talented**) singer will star in the new comedy show.

3. We made a quiet (**departure/unity**) so the baby wouldn't cry.

4. It takes great (**certainty/endurance**) to run a ten-mile race.

5. Lively music may chase away your (**gloom/variety**).

6. We made a careful (**exclamation/observation**) of the famous painting.

7. (**Loyalty/Sensitivity**) to certain foods means those foods might upset your stomach if you eat them.

8. The graceful cheetah is famous for its (**glances/swiftness**).

9. The ballerina performed (**fiercely/superbly**).

10. Smiling strangers often comment about the child's (**atmosphere/preciousness**).

Use the clue and the given letters to complete each word. Write the missing letters of the word in the appropriate boxes. Then use the circled letters and the drawing to answer the CHALLENGE question below.

1. To move around without a goal

| W | (⬭) | N | D | | |

2. Not showing much thought

| (⬭) | | | L | L | | |

3. To win someone over

| | | | V | | N | | (E) |

4. Wild or savage; very strong

| | I | | (⬭) | C | (⬭) |

5. Grab, seize, or catch

| | A | | (⬭) | (⬭) | R | |

6. A source of useful information

| (⬭) | | S | O | | R | | |

Challenge:

What do you think you might find inside the old trunk?

| | | | | | | | |

Definitions *Study the spelling, pronunciation, part of speech, and definition for each word. Write the word on the line in the sentence. Then read the synonyms and antonyms.*

1. **accuse**
   (ə 'kyüz)

   (v.) to say that someone or something has done wrong; blame

   Please don't _____ *me of being lazy!*

   SYNONYMS: blame, censure, tattle
   ANTONYMS: praise, absolve

2. **clever**
   ('kle vər)

   (adj.) having or showing a quick mind; bright, smart

   The _____ *student answered every question correctly.*

   SYNONYMS: smart, ingenious, intelligent, nimble, adroit, cunning
   ANTONYMS: dull, dumb, unintelligent, stupid, slow

3. **coast**
   (kōst)

   (n.) the land near the sea or ocean

   California is on the Pacific _____ *of the United States.*

   (v.) to move along without any power or effort; to slide down a slope

   Our sleds will _____ *down the hill.*

   SYNONYMS: (n.) seashore, seaside, waterfront, beach, bank;
   (v.) slide, glide, ride

4. **delicate**
   ('de li kət)

   (adj.) easily broken or damaged; requiring care or skill

   Do not touch that _____ *teacup, please!*

   SYNONYMS: dainty, fragile, weak, frail
   ANTONYMS: sturdy, hard, coarse, rough

5. **explore**
   (ik 'splôr)

   (v.) to travel; to discover; to look into or study something

   I would like to _____ *the new neighborhood.*

   SYNONYMS: examine, investigate, analyze, probe, search, research

The Statue of Liberty stands against the sky as a **symbol** (word 9) of freedom.

6. **imitate**
('i mə tāt)

(v.) to copy someone's movements or expressions; to appear like something else

I love to _____ the actors' funny faces.

SYNONYMS: copy, mimic, resemble, ape, repeat, emulate, reproduce

7. **pierce**
(pērs)

(v.) to make a hole or opening; to run into or through something, as with a pointed weapon

Use scissors to _____ the package.

SYNONYMS: stab, perforate, enter, penetrate

8. **rare**
(rar)

(adj.) not often found, seen, or happening; unusually valuable or good; not fully cooked

It is _____ for a pitcher to hit many home runs.

SYNONYMS: unusual, distinctive, choice, infrequent
ANTONYMS: ordinary, usual, common, normal, frequent

9. **symbol**
('sim bəl)

(n.) something that stands for something else; a written sign that is used to represent an operation or a calculation

A dove with an olive branch is a _____ of peace.

SYNONYMS: sign, mark, note, token, emblem, symptom

10. **triumph**
('trī əmf)

(n.) an important success or win; a feeling of happiness that comes from winning

Winning the battle was a _____ for them.

(v.) to succeed

The basketball team will _____ in the end.

SYNONYMS: (n.) victory, achievement; (v.) overcome, conquer
ANTONYMS: (n. & v.) defeat; (v.) frustrate, beat, destroy, lose

Match the Meaning

Choose the word whose meaning is suggested by the clue given. Then write the word on the line provided.

1. A strip of land along the water is called a _____.
   a. triumph b. symbol c. coast

2. Smart people may also be described as _____.
   a. rare b. clever c. delicate

3. To _____ is to go to a new or unknown place.
   a. imitate b. explore c. accuse

4. When you _____ people, you are saying they are doing something wrong.
   a. explore b. pierce c. accuse

5. Very unusual objects are said to be _____.
   a. rare b. clever c. delicate

6. To _____ people is to copy them.
   a. triumph b. imitate c. coast

7. A _____ might also be called a victory.
   a. triumph b. symbol c. coast

8. Something that is easily broken is _____.
   a. clever b. rare c. delicate

9. A pin might _____ a balloon.
   a. triumph b. pierce c. accuse

10. The mathematical _____ for addition is the plus sign.
    a. coast b. triumph c. symbol

Synonyms

*Choose the word that is most nearly the **same** in meaning as the word or phrase in **dark print**. Then write your choice on the line provided.*

1. the beauty of the **seashore**
   a. symbol   b. triumph   c. coast   _____

2. **investigate** the caves
   a. imitate   b. explore   c. pierce   _____

3. **mimic** my voice
   a. pierce   b. imitate   c. accuse   _____

4. **stab** the meat
   a. explore   b. coast   c. pierce   _____

5. **blame** the dog
   a. accuse   b. pierce   c. triumph   _____

6. a **sign** of freedom
   a. symbol   b. coast   c. triumph   _____

Antonyms

*Choose the word that is most nearly the **opposite** in meaning to the word or phrase in **dark print**. Then write your choice on the line provided.*

1. **slow** about details
   a. delicate   b. clever   c. rare   _____

2. **sturdy** glass plates
   a. clever   b. delicate   c. rare   _____

3. a surprising **defeat**
   a. triumph   b. coast   c. symbol   _____

4. a **common** complaint
   a. clever   b. delicate   c. rare   _____

Completing the Sentence *From the list of words on pages 42–43, choose the one that best completes each item below. Then write the word on the line provided. (You may have to change the word's ending.)*

Holidays

Holidays give people a chance to be creative and to think of
_____ costumes.

On Halloween this year, I'm going to dress up as my
favorite singer. I will _____ her.

When young children come to visit, Mom protects
our glasses by putting them on high shelves. Glasses
are _____ and break easily.

May Day is an important holiday in England. It is
_____, however, for Americans
to celebrate that holiday.

It is always good to _____ new
ways of making the holidays fun.

Politics

Candidates have to work very hard to get votes. If they
_____ along instead of working hard,
they will probably not win the election.

Unfortunately, it is common for candidates in a race to
_____ each other of not telling the truth.

Some politicians speak so loudly that their voices almost
_____ the air.

The _____ for the Republican Party is the donkey.
The sign of the Democratic Party is the elephant.

Usually, the candidate who loses the race congratulates the winner on
his or her _____.

*Circle the letter next to the choice that best completes the sentence or answers the question. Pay special attention to the word in **dark print**.*

1. If you **accuse** me, you might say,
   a. "It's all your fault."
   b. "Thanks for your help."
   c. "I'll take the blame."
   d. "You are in the clear."

2. It's **rare** to find a
   a. four-wheeled car.
   b. four-legged cat.
   c. four-room apartment.
   d. four-leaf clover.

3. Which tool is used to **pierce**?
   a. a paint brush
   b. a wrench
   c. a drill
   d. a ruler

4. A **delicate** object would be very easy to
   a. break.
   b. build.
   c. carry.
   d. copy.

5. To **imitate** a kangaroo, you might
   a. read and write.
   b. dance and sing.
   c. hop and wear a pouch.
   d. chirp and spread your arms like wings.

6. A race car could be a **symbol** of
   a. music.
   b. speed.
   c. food.
   d. hate.

7. If you live along the **coast** of Texas, you are probably
   a. a long way from the ocean.
   b. far from home.
   c. on a mountain top.
   d. near the water.

8. I **explore** if I go to a place I
   a. visit every day.
   b. know inside and out.
   c. have never been to before.
   d. think is no fun.

9. If you **triumph**, you are the
   a. loser.
   b. quitter.
   c. fighter.
   d. winner.

10. It takes a **clever** dog to
    a. bark at strangers.
    b. learn to "shake hands."
    c. chase cats and squirrels.
    d. chew on bones.

Definitions Study the spelling, pronunciation, part of speech, and definition for each word. Write the word on the line in the sentence. Then read the synonyms and antonyms.

1. **ancient**
   ('an shənt)

   (adj.) very old; early in history

   The fossil remains are _____.

   SYNONYMS: antique, old-fashioned, old, venerable
   ANTONYMS: new, recent

2. **climate**
   (klī mət)

   (n.) the usual weather conditions of a place

   I don't like that moist, hot _____.

   SYNONYMS: weather, atmosphere, environment, temperature

3. **cling**
   (kling)

   (v.) to hold on firmly; to have a strong attachment to or feeling for something or someone

   As a child, I used to _____ *to my mother.*

   SYNONYMS: hold, stick, attach, adhere, grasp
   ANTONYM: release

4. **custom**
   ('kəs təm)

   (n.) a common practice; the way people do things year after year

   It is a national _____ *to celebrate the Fourth of July.*

   SYNONYMS: tradition, habit

5. **decay**
   (di 'kā)

   (v.) to slowly decline or fall into ruin

   The salt water caused the dock to _____.

   (n.) the slow decline of something

   Go to the dentist twice a year to try to avoid tooth

   _____.

   SYNONYMS: (v.) ruin, rot, spoil, decompose, disintegrate, collapse, impair;
   (n.) weakening
   ANTONYMS: (v.) flourish, bloom

Eating turkey, cranberry sauce, and pumpkin pie is a **custom** (word 4) celebrated by many people on Thanksgiving.

6. **disturb**
(di 'stərb)

(v.) to make upset or uneasy

We tried not to _____ their sleep.

SYNONYMS: interrupt, stop, disrupt, alarm, discompose
ANTONYMS: calm, soothe

7. **expose**
(ik 'spōz)

(v.) to uncover or open to view; to make something known

I promise not to _____ their secrets.

SYNONYMS: show, reveal, disclose, display, uncover
ANTONYMS: cover, hide, disguise, mask

8. **perform**
(pər 'fôrm)

(v.) to carry out a task; to act or entertain

They were asked to _____ the play on Wednesday.

SYNONYMS: achieve, fulfill, do, act, function, present, play

9. **remote**
(ri 'mōt)

(adj.) far removed in distance or time, out of the way; unlikely; very slight

We drove to a _____ cabin in the woods.

SYNONYMS: far, divergent, secluded
ANTONYMS: near, nearby, open

10. **timid**
('ti məd)

(adj.) lacking courage or confidence

I was too _____ to talk to the new teacher.

SYNONYMS: cautious, shy, cowardly, meek
ANTONYMS: bold, brash, daring, determined, confident

Match the Meaning

Choose the word whose meaning is suggested by the clue given. Then write the word on the line provided.

1. To interrupt a conversation is to _____ it.
   a. cling   b. decay   c. disturb

2. A(n) _____ place is far away.
   a. ancient   b. timid   c. remote

3. Something very old is considered _____.
   a. timid   b. ancient   c. remote

4. The _____ of a region refers to its weather patterns.
   a. custom   b. climate   c. decay

5. To _____ is to hold on tightly.
   a. cling   b. perform   c. expose

6. If you _____ something, you uncover it.
   a. decay   b. perform   c. expose

7. A(n) _____ person lacks confidence and courage.
   a. timid   b. remote   c. ancient

8. To put on a show is to _____.
   a. cling   b. perform   c. disturb

9. A _____ is an event that is repeated regularly.
   a. climate   b. decay   c. custom

10. The decline of something means its _____.
    a. decay   b. custom   c. climate

*Choose the word that is most nearly the **same** in meaning as the word or phrase in **dark print**. Then write your choice on the line provided.*

1. **fulfill** your duties
   a. cling   b. perform   c. decay   _____

2. meat that has **spoiled**
   a. clung   b. decayed   c. disturbed   _____

3. **hold on** to the wall
   a. cling   b. decay   c. expose   _____

4. the city's **weather**
   a. decay   b. custom   c. climate   _____

5. a family's **tradition**
   a. custom   b. climate   c. decay   _____

6. news that **upsets**
   a. clings   b. performs   c. disturbs   _____

Antonyms

*Choose the word that is most nearly the **opposite** in meaning to the word or phrase in **dark print**. Then write your choice on the line provided.*

1. a **new** item
   a. ancient   b. remote   c. timid   _____

2. a **nearby** road
   a. timid   b. ancient   c. remote   _____

3. a **bold** reaction
   a. remote   b. ancient   c. timid   _____

4. **cover** the wound
   a. cling   b. expose   c. perform   _____

From the list of words on pages 48–49, choose the one that best completes each item below. Then write the word on the line provided. (You may have to change the word's ending.)

Gorillas and Their Environment

Many gorillas live in jungles and tropical rain forests.

The _____ of a tropical rain forest is very wet, with very high temperatures.

Young gorillas _____ to their mothers' backs when traveling in the jungle.

Female gorillas may seem more _____ than males, but in fact they are just as brave.

Gorillas sleep for a few hours after they eat. It is wise not to _____ them while they sleep!

Our Theater

Welcome to our theater! I know it looks old and in a state of _____, but I promise you that it will stand up just fine!

This theater was once a beautiful place. Just push back the curtains to _____ the lovely murals.

This evening, we will _____ a show for you.

Every year, it is our _____ to put on a show celebrating different countries.

This play is based on an _____ Egyptian myth. It is a very old story of how the earth was born.

I know the chances that I'll become a great star are _____. If that does happen, however, I will be happy to share my secrets of success!

Word Associations

*Circle the letter next to the choice that best completes the sentence or answers the question. Pay special attention to the word in **dark print**.*

1. Which is **ancient**?
   a. a computer
   b. a bicycle
   c. a puppy
   d. a mummy

2. A **custom** is something you
   a. do on a regular basis.
   b. don't like to do.
   c. are forced to do.
   d. don't do at all.

3. To **expose** house plants to light, you might put them
   a. near a window.
   b. in a closet.
   c. under the bed.
   d. on a table.

4. A **timid** person might try to
   a. show off.
   b. make a speech.
   c. be a hero.
   d. shy away from a group.

5. When an apple starts to **decay**, it
   a. tastes sweet and juicy.
   b. gets brown and mushy.
   c. is fresh and crispy.
   d. needs to be washed.

6. People who study the **climate** of a place pay attention to
   a. its people.
   b. its weather.
   c. its traffic.
   d. its cities.

7. If I **disturb** you, I should say,
   a. "Have you read a good book?"
   b. "Will you come to my party?"
   c. "Excuse me for bothering you."
   d. "Please take a bath."

8. To **perform** a task, you must
   a. finish it.
   b. stay away from it.
   c. quit before the end.
   d. ask an adult for help.

9. A **remote** cabin would have
   a. many rooms.
   b. many visitors.
   c. few neighbors.
   d. many houses nearby.

10. If you **cling** to an idea, you
    a. stick to it.
    b. forget it.
    c. ignore it.
    d. change your mind.

Definitions *Study the spelling, pronunciation, part of speech, and definition for each word. Write the word on the line in the sentence. Then read the synonyms and antonyms.*

1. ability
(ə 'bi lə tē)

(n.) the power or skill to do something

Lifeguards must have the _____ to swim well.

SYNONYMS: aptitude, coordination, dexterity, skill
ANTONYMS: inability, powerlessness

2. avoid
(ə 'void)

(v.) to keep away from

They tried to _____ the mud slide, but they were not successful.

SYNONYMS: evade, escape, elude, shun
ANTONYM: seek

3. bashful
('bash fůl)

(adj.) shy, not at ease, especially in a social setting

Why were you so _____ at the party?

SYNONYMS: timid, shy, reserved, diffident, hesitant, self-conscious, awkward, uneasy
ANTONYMS: bold, brash, aggressive, forward, extroverted, outgoing

4. brief
(brēf)

(adj.) short in time, amount, or length

A three-day vacation is too _____ for me.

SYNONYMS: quick, short, fleeting, concise, curt, pithy, succinct, terse
ANTONYMS: long, lengthy, extended

5. compete
(kəm 'pēt)

(v.) to try for something, such as a prize; to take part in a game or contest; to play against another or others

In gym, students might _____ in the 50-yard dash.

SYNONYMS: strive, rival, vie with, contend, challenge

Five children **compete** (word 5) in a 50-yard dash.

6. **consider**
   (kən 'sid ər)

   (v.) to think about or pay attention to

   Be sure to _____ your choices carefully.

   SYNONYMS: think, weigh, analyze, evaluate, ponder, reflect, regard, study
   ANTONYMS: decline, rebuff, reject, repel

7. **delightful**
   (di 'līt fəl)

   (adj.) very pleasing, wonderful

   Going to a carnival is a _____ experience.

   SYNONYMS: lovely, appealing, enjoyable, agreeable, pleasant, joyful
   ANTONYMS: disagreeable, displeasing, unpleasant, joyless

8. **honor**
   ('ä nər)

   (n.) great respect; a sign of respect; a sense of what is right

   They sent a card in _____ of my birthday.

   (v.) to respect or value

   Will you _____ my request for an allowance?

   SYNONYMS: (n. & v.) praise, credit, esteem; (n.) glory, recognition, reputation, integrity, prestige, privilege
   ANTONYMS: (n. & v.) disgrace, dishonor; (v.) humiliate

9. **reflex**
   ('rē fleks)

   (n.) an automatic response, usually very quick

   My _____ is to jump at the sight of a spider.

   SYNONYM: response

10. **remark**
    (ri 'märk)

    (n.) a short statement

    That was an unkind _____ about their old shoes.

    (v.) to say, mention; give an opinion

    Ask them to _____ on the shape of the clouds.

    SYNONYMS: (n. & v.) comment; (n.) observation, statement; (v.) observe, say, speak, state, mention

Match the Meaning

Choose the word whose meaning is suggested by the clue given. Then write the word on the line provided.

1. A quick reaction is a(n) _____.
   a. ability   b. reflex   c. honor

2. A person who has the skill to do something has the _____ to do it.
   a. remark   b. honor   c. ability

3. When I make a(n) _____, I am commenting on something.
   a. remark   b. ability   c. honor

4. To _____ something is to stay away from it.
   a. compete   b. consider   c. avoid

5. A _____ speech is a short one.
   a. bashful   b. brief   c. delightful

6. When people are afraid to speak up, they might be _____.
   a. bashful   b. brief   c. delightful

7. To _____ taking an action is to think about doing it.
   a. compete   b. consider   c. avoid

8. To _____ in a race is to take part in it.
   a. avoid   b. remark   c. compete

9. A person who is well respected receives much _____.
   a. ability   b. reflex   c. honor

10. The long vacation was enjoyable and _____.
    a. delightful   b. bashful   c. brief

Synonyms

*Choose the word that is most nearly the **same** in meaning as the word or phrase in **dark print**. Then write your choice on the line provided.*

1. **escape** the bad weather
   a. compete   b. consider   c. avoid   _____

2. **strive** for the best
   a. consider   b. compete   c. remark   _____

3. a **self-conscious** newcomer
   a. bashful   b. brief   c. delightful   _____

4. a nasty **comment**
   a. honor   b. remark   c. reflex   _____

5. **study** the test results
   a. avoid   b. compete   c. consider   _____

6. a quick **response**
   a. ability   b. reflex   c. remark   _____

Antonyms

*Choose the word that is most nearly the **opposite** in meaning to the word or phrase in **dark print**. Then write your choice on the line provided.*

1. a **lengthy** conversation
   a. brief   b. bashful   c. delightful   _____

2. the **disagreeable** situation
   a. brief   b. delightful   c. bashful   _____

3. **humiliate** the person
   a. avoid   b. honor   c. remark   _____

4. a **powerlessness** to understand
   a. honor   b. ability   c. reflex   _____

From the list of words on pages 54–55, choose the one that best completes each item below. Then write the word on the line provided. (You may have to change the word's ending.)

My Pets

My parents often _____ on how well I take care of my dog and cat, saying that I treat my pets very well.

Each of my pets has different _____. One talent that my cat has is that she has great _____. She reacts and moves very quickly!

My cat is sometimes _____.
At times, she hides from strangers, the way a shy child might.

I love to watch my dog play with other dogs. It's fun to watch the dogs _____
for a big bone or a ball, bumping into each other as each one tries to get the object.

Once in a while, I come home from school and am very tired. I'm just not in the mood to play with my dog and cat! On those days, I almost feel like _____ my pets.

But I always make sure to spend some time with them. Even a _____ amount of time with them is better than no time at all!

I love my cat and dog. They are both charming and _____. It is (an) _____
to have them as pets!

Which animal do you _____
to be the better pet? You have to decide that for yourself!

Word Associations

*Circle the letter next to the choice that best completes the sentence or answers the question. Pay special attention to the word in **dark print**.*

1. To **avoid** getting wet, you might
   a. take a shower.
   b. bathe the dog.
   c. splash in a puddle.
   d. carry an umbrella.

2. When I **consider** the results of my actions, I try to
   a. pay no attention to what I'm doing.
   b. think ahead.
   c. not think at all.
   d. do what I want.

3. Which is a great **honor**?
   a. being chosen for an award
   b. being ignored
   c. making a telephone call
   d. getting a headache

4. A **delightful** time makes me feel
   a. dark and gloomy.
   b. angry and sad.
   c. joyful and happy.
   d. bored and restless.

5. A **brief** visit would last for
   a. two years.
   b. five months.
   c. ten weeks.
   d. three minutes.

6. When you **compete**, you try hard
   a. to win.
   b. to smile.
   c. to lose.
   d. to relax.

7. Someone with good **reflexes**
   a. moves slowly.
   b. moves quickly.
   c. thinks slowly.
   d. doesn't react at all.

8. If I ask you to **remark** on my story, I want you to
   a. rewrite it.
   b. make fun of it.
   c. tell me what you think of it.
   d. write your own story.

9. "What **ability**!" the teacher says. The teacher thinks the child is
   a. talented.
   b. lazy.
   c. bored.
   d. weak.

10. At the party, a **bashful** child would
   a. greet each guest with a grin.
   b. make new friends easily.
   c. feel nervous and shy.
   d. play the piano for the guests.

Definitions *Study the spelling, pronunciation, part of speech, and definition for each word. Write the word on the line in the sentence. Then read the synonyms and antonyms.*

1. **actual**
   ('ak chü wəl)

   (adj.) happening in fact or reality

   My party is three days after my _____ birthday.

   SYNONYMS: real, true, factual, genuine, authentic, legitimate, existing
   ANTONYMS: false, untrue, unreal, nonexistent

2. **brink**
   (brink)

   (n.) the highest point of a steep place; the very edge, verge

   We stood near the _____ of the cliff.

   SYNONYMS: edge, verge, point, border, threshold

3. **chill**
   (chil)

   (n.) an unpleasant feeling of coldness, often from illness or fear

   I felt a _____ as I skated on the pond.

   (v.) to make or become cold

   The recipe suggests to _____ the dessert.

   SYNONYMS: (n.) coldness, coolness, nip; (v.) cool, refrigerate, freeze
   ANTONYMS: (n. & v.) heat; (n.) warmth; (v.) defrost; warm

4. **conquer**
   ('kän kər)

   (v.) to defeat or take over; to master or overcome

   The army hoped to _____ the enemy overnight.

   SYNONYMS: win, defeat, beat, overpower, overthrow, overcome, control, excel, vanquish
   ANTONYMS: surrender, yield, submit, relinquish

5. **fortunate**
   ('fôr chə nət)

   (adj.) having or bringing good luck; lucky

   We were _____ to have no rain during spring break.

   SYNONYMS: lucky, blessed, happy, successful, auspicious, favorable, fortuitous, propitious
   ANTONYMS: unfortunate, unlucky, unfavorable, inauspicious

A hiker enjoys the view standing at the **brink** (word 2) of a cliff.

6. **fury**
('fyùr ē)

(n.) strong anger, rage

A bad temper often leads to a state of _____.

SYNONYMS: anger, rage, wrath, fierceness, violence, force, power

7. **intend**
(in 'tend)

(v.) to plan to do something; to have a goal or purpose

I hope you _____ *to do your homework.*

SYNONYMS: plan, mean, aim, expect, propose

8. **pattern**
('pa tərn)

(n.) the way that shapes and colors are put together; a model or guide for making something; a design that is repeated

The striped _____ *is the same in each candy cane.*

(v.) to make or follow according to a model or design

I hope to _____ *my behavior after someone I look up to.*

SYNONYMS: (n. & v.) model, style, form; (n.) design, system, order, arrangement, sequence, guide, standard; (v.) imitate, match

9. **vibrant**
('vī brənt)

(adj.) full of life, energy, or activity

Your personality is lively and _____.

SYNONYMS: lively, energetic, spirited, dynamic, vivid, bright, striking
ANTONYMS: listless, lifeless, dull, inconspicuous, ordinary, unremarkable

10. **wit**
(wit)

(n.) the talent to describe things or people in a funny or unusual way; the ability to think clearly; a clever and amusing person

A teacher with _____ *often knows how to keep the students' attention in class.*

SYNONYMS: humor, intelligence, cleverness, acumen, ingenuity
ANTONYMS: stupidity, seriousness

Match the Meaning

Choose the word whose meaning is suggested by the clue given. Then write the word on the line provided.

1. A _____ is a design that repeats.
   a. wit   b. brink   c. pattern

2. Something that is true or real is _____.
   a. actual   b. vibrant   c. fortunate

3. When you are just about to begin a task, you are on the _____ of doing it.
   a. brink   b. chill   c. fury

4. A funny person is also sometimes called a _____.
   a. pattern   b. wit   c. brink

5. When you make something cold, you _____ it.
   a. conquer   b. pattern   c. chill

6. Something _____ is full of life.
   a. actual   b. vibrant   c. fortunate

7. If you are _____, you have good luck.
   a. actual   b. fortunate   c. vibrant

8. To overcome a tough situation is to _____ it.
   a. conquer   b. chill   c. intend

9. A very angry person has much _____.
   a. brink   b. wit   c. fury

10. To _____ to finish a project is to plan to do it.
    a. chill   b. conquer   c. intend

Synonyms

*Choose the word that is most nearly the **same** in meaning as the word or phrase in **dark print**. Then write your choice on the line provided.*

1. hang over the **edge**
   a. fury   b. brink   c. pattern   _____

2. the tiger's **rage**
   a. wit   b. chill   c. fury   _____

3. showing great **intelligence**
   a. brink   b. wit   c. pattern   _____

4. a gorgeous **design**
   a. pattern   b. chill   c. fury   _____

5. **plan** to see us
   a. intend   b. chill   c. conquer   _____

Antonyms

*Choose the word that is most nearly the **opposite** in meaning to the word or phrase in **dark print**. Then write your choice on the line provided.*

1. a **false** occurrence
   a. vibrant   b. actual   c. fortunate   _____

2. **warm up** the dessert
   a. chill   b. conquer   c. pattern   _____

3. an **unlucky** person
   a. actual   b. vibrant   c. fortunate   _____

4. **submit to** the warrior
   a. conquer   b. pattern   c. intend   _____

5. a **dull** story
   a. actual   b. fortunate   c. vibrant   _____

Completing the Sentence

From the list of words on pages 60–61, choose the one that best completes each item below. Then write the word on the line provided. (You may have to change the word's ending.)

Books

I read every book the same way. My reading _____ is to find a book, put my feet up, and turn to the first page.

I like reading biographies because I know that I am reading the _____ facts of a person's life.

I love authors who put _____ into their stories and make me laugh out loud.

Some mystery books are so good that reading them can send _____ up my spine.

I am on the _____ of finishing a great mystery novel. The two main characters in this book have been accused of committing a crime. I think they are both innocent!

The books that I enjoy most are those that are fun to read and have a _____ writing style.

My favorite author is Roald Dahl. I like *Jimmy and the Giant Peach* so much that I _____ to read it again this weekend.

Water, Water Everywhere

One way that people have tried to _____ the endless flow of rivers is to build dams, levees, and reservoirs.

People who live in areas of high rainfall are _____. They are lucky that they never have to worry about getting enough water.

There is nothing that compares to the _____ of a hurricane.

Word Associations

*Circle the letter next to the choice that best completes the sentence or answers the question. Pay special attention to the word in **dark print.***

1. A story of **actual** people is about
   a. made-up characters.
   b. persons who never existed.
   c. real persons.
   d. aliens or robots.

2. "I **intend** to go bowling" means
   a. I never want to do that activity.
   b. I plan to try that sport.
   c. I'm afraid to try bowling.
   d. I don't know what bowling is.

3. If the Bugs **conquer** the Bees, you can say that
   a. the Bugs win.
   b. the Bees win.
   c. the Bugs lose.
   d. it's a tie game.

4. A **vibrant** poem is one that
   a. always rhymes.
   b. sounds like all the others.
   c. is exciting.
   d. is boring.

5. One way to **chill** a drink is to
   a. add ice cubes to it.
   b. boil it for five minutes.
   c. sprinkle salt into it.
   d. pour it into a jar.

6. A song with **wit** might make you
   a. cry.
   b. laugh.
   c. forget the words.
   d. cover your ears.

7. Which comment shows **fury**?
   a. "What a tasty dessert!"
   b. "Sweet dreams, dear."
   c. "That's a beautiful sweater!"
   d. "I could wring their necks!"

8. Being on the **brink** of tears means that you are
   a. combing your hair.
   b. finished crying.
   c. about to start crying.
   d. standing on a cliff.

9. You'd probably feel **fortunate** if
   a. you got caught in the rain.
   b. you scraped your knee.
   c. you found a $10 bill.
   d. you lost your wallet.

10. A dress with a **pattern** has a
    a. long zipper.
    b. repeating design.
    c. shiny belt.
    d. roomy pocket.

Selecting Word Meanings

*Circle the choice that is most nearly the **same** in meaning as the word in **dark print**.*

1. **clings to** the branch
   a. climbs   b. drops   c. holds   d. breaks

2. to **decay** in a muddy swamp
   a. rot   b. swim   c. hide   d. stick

3. heard that funny **remark**
   a. poem   b. comment   c. speech   d. custom

4. hope to **conquer** this disease
   a. catch   b. describe   c. imitate   d. defeat

5. the **pattern** of a chess board
   a. cost   b. pieces   c. design   d. price

6. like a **delicate** flower
   a. dainty   b. drooping   c. favorite   d. dying

7. a **symbol** of love
   a. candy   b. memory   c. token   d. poem

8. mild **climate**
   a. food   b. manner   c. temper   d. temperature

9. to **honor** their wishes
   a. ignore   b. avoid   c. repeat   d. respect

10. shook with **fury**
   a. fear   b. anger   c. fever   d. cold

Spelling

*Study the word in **dark print**. If a letter is missing, fill in the blank to make a correctly spelled word. If the word is already spelled correctly, leave the blank empty.*

1. **vi__rant** colors

2. great **abil__ity**

3. **im__tate** a clown

4. quick **r__flex**

5. **tri__mph** over the enemy

6. **inten__** to call

7. **p__erce** the air

8. **an__ient** writing

9. a weekly **cust__om**

10. to **avo__d** sneezing

Antonyms

*Circle the choice that is most nearly the **opposite** in meaning as the word in **dark print**.*

1. **accuse** the person
   a. blame   b. praise   c. discuss   d. ask

2. the **timid** new student
   a. shy   b. smart   c. lucky   d. confident

3. gave a **brief** speech
   a. serious   b. short   c. lengthy   d. loud

4. **chill** the baby's bottle
   a. warm   b. empty   c. fill   d. cool

5. has such **delightful** memories
   a. lovely   b. distant   c. unpleasant   d. old

Vocabulary in Context

Words have been left out of the following passage. For each numbered item in the passage, fill in the circle next to the word in the margin that best fills the blank space.

Can you imagine living all by yourself on a __1__ island far from home? A book written nearly 300 years ago is based on this idea. The book has a very long title. But most people simply know it as the story of Robinson Crusoe.

1. ○ bashful
   ○ remote
   ○ nearby
   ○ fortunate

Robinson Crusoe leaves home to go to sea. One day, a bad storm hits, and his ship is wrecked. Everyone on board drowns except for Crusoe. The rough sea batters him, leaving Crusoe at the __2__ of death. He finally washes up on a small island. He is scared and hurt, but he is alive.

2. ○ center
   ○ custom
   ○ end
   ○ brink

Robinson Crusoe may be alive, but he is still in big trouble. He searches the island for help, but he finds no one. Now he has to __3__ new problems. How will he survive all alone? How will Crusoe find food? What will he do for shelter? Will anyone ever come to save him? He survives many adventures. He uses his __4__ every day. Crusoe stays on his island for 28 long years. In the end, some pirates find him. They bring him home at last.

3. ○ consider
   ○ imitate
   ○ honor
   ○ gather

4. ○ patterns
   ○ charts
   ○ wits
   ○ symbols

People say that this story came from real life. The person who wrote the story of Robinson Crusoe based it on something that really happened. The __5__ event happened to a sailor named Alexander Selkirk. He and his captain had a fight at sea. Selkirk asked to be dropped off on a tiny island. The captain agreed to do this. Like Crusoe, Selkirk lived alone. But Selkirk stayed on his island for only five years!

5. ○ delightful
   ○ vibrant
   ○ ancient
   ○ actual

Analogies

Circle the item that best completes the comparison. Then explain the relationship on the line provided.

1. **timid** is to **bashful** as
   a. dance is to sing
   b. paper is to wood
   c. minute is to hour
   d. ancient is to old

   Relationship: _____

   _____

   _____

3. **clever** is to **wit** as
   a. expose is to hide
   b. pattern is to needle
   c. vibrant is to energy
   d. glass is to break

   Relationship: _____

   _____

   _____

2. **actual** is to **unreal** as
   a. fortunate is to unlucky
   b. decay is to ruin
   c. school is to book
   d. true is to honest

   Relationship: _____

   _____

   _____

4. **compete** is to **contest** as
   a. win is to lose
   b. play is to game
   c. war is to triumph
   d. joke is to wit

   Relationship: _____

   _____

   _____

Challenge: Make up your own

Write a comparison using the words in the box. (Hint: There may be more than one possible answer.) Then explain the relationship on the lines provided.

cover	expose	hide	show

Analogy: _____ is to _____ as _____ is to _____.

Relationship: _____

_____

 **Word Families**

*The words in **dark print** in the sentences below are related to words introduced in Units 5–8. For example, the adverbs timidly and vibrantly in Item 1 are related to the adjectives timid (Unit 6) and vibrant (Unit 8). Circle the related word in **dark print** that best completes each sentence.*

accuse	clever	explore	perform	timid
avoid	compete	fury	pierce	triumph
brief	custom	honor	rare	vibrant
chill	disturb	imitate	symbol	wit

1. The frightened child curled up **(timidly/vibrantly)** in the corner.

2. We saw the very first **(imitation/performance)** of the new ballet.

3. Careful driving can make many accidents **(honorable/avoidable)**.

4. Luckily, the sound of the **(piercing/symbolic)** siren alerted us at once.

5. The **(witty/furious)** mob threw rocks and bottles at the enemy.

6. The chess **(accusation/competition)** turned out to be very close.

7. A heavy snowstorm in July would be quite a **(cleverness/rarity)**.

8. The winner's **(chilly/triumphant)** speech made the fans leap to their feet.

9. I **(briefly/customarily)** have cereal and fruit for breakfast on school days.

10. Phone calls during dinner are an annoying **(disturbance/exploration)**.

Be a word hunter! Ten words from Units 5–8 are hidden in the grid below. Five of them go across. Five go from top to bottom. Find and circle all ten words.

C	O	N	S	I	D	E	R	U	G
H	O	U	Z	E	I	X	D	I	J
I	Q	C	O	A	S	T	J	O	W
L	B	R	K	H	T	I	M	I	D
L	D	E	G	U	U	F	W	P	C
Y	R	F	I	W	R	S	L	I	M
D	F	L	R	J	B	B	Q	E	K
W	L	E	A	S	G	F	U	R	Y
Q	P	X	R	K	N	H	L	C	T
P	O	E	E	X	P	O	S	E	M

From the words circled above, choose the five that best complete the sentences below. Write those words on the lines provided.

1. "If you feel a _____, you should put on a hat," said Mel.

2. "Did you _____ how that would mess up my hair?" asked Nell.

3. "Yes, but if you _____ yourself to the cold, you'll get sick," said Mel.

4. "It's _____ for me to get sick," said Nell. "I'm always so healthy."

5. "But if you do get sick, it will _____ our plans," said Mel.

Definitions

Choose the word from the box that matches each definition. Write the word on the line provided. The first one has been done for you.

accuse	endure	superb
ancient	gasp	timid
brief	plunge	unite
brink	sensitive	~~value~~
coward	shatter	wisdom

1. the worth of something; an amount   value

2. to say that someone or something has done wrong   _____

3. to quickly throw one's self down or into something   _____

4. knowledge and good sense   _____

5. very old; early in history   _____

6. to break into many pieces; to cause much damage   _____

7. short in time, amount, or length   _____

8. to put up with; continue the same way for a long time   _____

9. the highest point of a steep place   _____

10. reacting to something quickly; easily hurt or bothered   _____

Antonyms

*Choose the word from the box that is most nearly **opposite** in meaning to each group of words. Write the word on the line provided. The first one has been done for you.*

1. stay, remain   _____wander_____

2. sturdy, coarse, rough   _____

3. worthless, valueless, ordinary   _____

4. undo, loosen, detach, unfasten   _____

5. frustrate, defeat, destroy, lose   _____

6. flourish, bloom   _____

7. bold, brash, aggressive, forward,
   outgoing   _____

8. unfavorable, unlucky   _____

9. false, unreal, untrue   _____

10. decline, rebuff, reject, repel   _____

11. near, nearby, open   _____

12. mild, easygoing, placid   _____

13. inability, powerlessness   _____

14. foolish, dull, unintelligent   _____

15. slow, lazy, passive   _____

ability
active
actual
bashful
clasp
clever
consider
decay
delicate
fierce
fortunate
precious
remote
triumph
~~wander~~

 **Completing the Sentence**

Choose the word from the box that best completes each sentence below. Write the word on the line provided. The first one has been done for you.

Group A

atmosphere	~~bargains~~	border
capture	endures	sensitive

1. They found many wonderful _____**bargains**_____ at the second-hand sale.

2. We took many pictures to _____ the fun of the baby's first party.

3. I felt very uneasy in the dusty, stale _____ of the old shack.

4. They made a simple _____ for the yard by planting rows of flowers.

Group B

cling	explore	honor
intend	perform	remark

1. Someday, I would love to _____ the lovely beaches of Kauai.

2. I can't wait to see you _____ three new magic tricks for our guests.

3. I meant it as a casual _____, so I'm sorry that you took it the wrong way.

4. They _____ to walk the dog as soon as it stops raining.

Classifying

Choose the word from the box that goes best with each group of words. Write the word on the line provided. Then explain what the words have in common. The first one has been done for you.

disturb	exclaim	gasp	glance
~~journey~~	rare	swift	wander

1. cruise, vacation, voyage, _____**journey**_____

   The words name kinds of trips. _____

2. inhale, pant, wheeze, _____

   _____

3. quick, rapid, speedy, _____

   _____

4. _____ , walk, skip, run

   _____

5. _____ , disturbing, disturbance

   _____

6. whisper, declare, shout, _____

   _____

7. _____ , look, stare

   _____

8. fair, spare, there, _____

   _____

Definitions

Study the spelling, pronunciation, part of speech, and definition for each word. Write the word on the line in the sentence. Then read the synonyms and antonyms.

1. **approach**
   (ə 'prōch)

   (v.) to come close to; to begin to deal with; to make a request

   We watched the train _____ the station.

   (n.) the act of coming close to; a way to deal with something or someone; a way of reaching a place

   The _____ of spring makes many people giddy.

   SYNONYMS: (v. & n.) access; (v.) near; undertake; (n.) manner, method, system, technique, attitude, style; entrance, avenue, route
   ANTONYMS: (v.) leave, avoid, retreat

2. **approve**
   (ə 'prüv)

   (v.) to have a high opinion of; to give permission

   My parents _____ of my loyal friends.

   SYNONYMS: accept, admire; agree to, accredit, endorse, authorize
   ANTONYMS: reject, condemn, disapprove, discredit

3. **glory**
   ('glôr ē)

   (n.) great honor or praise given by others; great beauty

   Can anything match the _____ of a sunset?

   SYNONYMS: honor, praise, fame; beauty, splendor, magnificence
   ANTONYMS: shame; disgrace, dishonor, obscurity; ugliness

4. **magnificent**
   (mag 'ni fə sənt)

   (adj.) very grand and fine; remarkably beautiful or outstanding

   The White House is a _____ building.

   SYNONYMS: superb, majestic, striking, splendid, glorious, imposing, impressive
   ANTONYMS: ordinary, plain, simple, modest, poor

5. **meek**
   (mēk)

   (adj.) not courageous or strong

   I felt _____ and did not speak loudly enough.

   SYNONYMS: mild, gentle, easygoing, quiet; weak, timid, submissive
   ANTONYMS: brave, bold, outgoing, outspoken, assertive, aggressive, overbearing; strong, courageous

The **magnificent** (word 4) Taj Mahal in India is one of the most beautiful buildings in the world.

6. **prompt**
(prämpt)

(adj.) on time; done quickly and without delay

They answered the invitation in a _____ manner.

(v.) to move someone to action; to remind someone what to do or what to say

I had to _____ my friend to make the call.

SYNONYMS: (adj.) early, punctual, timely; fast, quick; (v.) cause, make, urge, encourage, motivate, stimulate; remind, cue
ANTONYMS: (adj.) slow, late, tardy, delayed; (v.) discourage, deter

7. **revive**
(ri 'vīv)

(v.) to bring or come back to life

The nurse tried to _____ the patient.

SYNONYMS: resuscitate, renew, restore, return
ANTONYMS: deaden, impair, kill

8. **tradition**
(trə 'di shən)

(n.) a custom, belief, or idea that has been passed down over time

Trust in democracy is an American _____.

SYNONYMS: custom, pattern, practice, ritual

9. **watchful**
('wäch fəl)

(adj.) always noticing what is happening, aware

A scout must be silent and _____.

SYNONYMS: alert, aware, observant, vigilant
ANTONYMS: sleepy, unaware, oblivious

10. **wreckage**
('re kij)

(n.) what is left of something that has been destroyed

The _____ of the car was taken away.

SYNONYMS: ruins, remains, remnants, destruction

Match the Meaning

Choose the word whose meaning is suggested by the clue given. Then write the word on the line provided.

1. A _____ object might also be described as splendid.
   a. meek   b. magnificent   c. prompt

2. When you give an okay to a job, you _____ it.
   a. revive   b. approach   c. approve

3. To lack courage is to be _____.
   a. magnificent   b. meek   c. watchful

4. A(n) _____ to a highway brings you close to it.
   a. wreckage   b. glory   c. approach

5. The remains of an explosion is often called the _____.
   a. wreckage   b. approach   c. glory

6. A(n) _____ is a custom that is passed down.
   a. approach   b. tradition   c. glory

7. To _____ someone is to bring that person back to life.
   a. approve   b. approach   c. revive

8. To be _____ is to be awake and alert.
   a. watchful   b. prompt   c. magnificent

9. People who are _____ are known to be on time.
   a. magnificent   b. watchful   c. prompt

10. Those who want great honor may want a lot of _____.
    a. glory   b. tradition   c. wreckage

*Choose the word that is most nearly the **same** in meaning as the word or phrase in **dark print**. Then write your choice on the line provided.*

1. **resuscitate** the patient
   a. approach   b. approve   c. revive   _____

2. an old-fashioned **ritual**
   a. wreckage   b. approach   c. tradition   _____

3. **near** the finish line
   a. approach   b. revive   c. approve   _____

4. give **praise** to the winner
   a. glory   b. approach   c. wreckage   _____

5. **endorse** the new test
   a. approach   b. revive   c. approve   _____

6. clean up the **ruins**
   a. glory   b. wreckage   c. tradition   _____

Antonyms

*Choose the word that is most nearly the **opposite** in meaning to the word or phrase in **dark print**. Then write your choice on the line provided.*

1. a **plain** couch
   a. meek   b. magnificent   c. prompt   _____

2. a **strong** reaction to the insult
   a. watchful   b. meek   c. magnificent   _____

3. a **sleepy** guard
   a. magnificent   b. prompt   c. watchful   _____

4. **discourage** the decision
   a. prompt   b. glory   c. tradition   _____

From the list of words on pages 76–77, choose the one that best completes each item below. Then write the word on the line provided. (You may have to change the word's ending.)

Ancient Rome

The Roman gods received much _____ and honor because they were believed to have incredible powers and strengths.

No expense was spared in building the _____ temples where these gods were honored.

The destruction of Rome resulted in the _____ of these temples. Today we see only their ruins.

It would not be a good idea to _____ the ancient Roman custom of having gladiators fight lions in coliseums.

The Spanish custom of bullfighting is modeled after that early Roman _____.

School Lunch

Our teachers do not _____ of bad manners in the cafeteria.

They are _____ of us as we carry our trays to our tables. They want to make sure there are no accidents and that no child gets hurt.

In the rush to get in line for the hot lunch, _____ children often end up being the last to get their lunches.

Today, our class was the first class to _____ the doors of the cafeteria. That put us at the beginning of the line.

Classes that are _____ and finish their lunch on time get to go out for recess.

Word Associations

*Circle the letter next to the choice that best completes the sentence or answers the question. Pay special attention to the word in **dark print**.*

1. If you **approve** of the restaurant, it is likely that you will
   a. hate the food you order.
   b. like the food you order.
   c. argue with the waiter.
   d. argue over the bill.

2. In a quarrel, a **meek** child might
   a. make strong arguments.
   b. refuse to give in.
   c. yell and scream.
   d. not speak up at all.

3. A **magnificent** hotel would have
   a. lumpy beds and broken chairs.
   b. fancy rooms and a grand lobby.
   c. small, plain guest rooms.
   d. poor guest service.

4. You might see **wreckage** after
   a. the street cleaners come.
   b. a jet plane takes off.
   c. a building is torn down.
   d. you go to the movies.

5. **Prompt** guests will probably be
   a. angry.
   b. annoying.
   c. on time.
   d. delayed.

6. It is an old **tradition** in our school to have
   a. a field day every June.
   b. teachers in the classroom.
   c. windows in every room.
   d. a telephone number.

7. As I **approach** the lake, it
   a. appears to be farther away.
   b. is harder to see.
   c. seems smaller.
   d. appears to be closer.

8. To **revive** an old car, you must
   a. make it run again.
   b. call an ambulance.
   c. learn to drive.
   d. sell it.

9. A **watchful** clerk
   a. chats with customers.
   b. daydreams a lot.
   c. doesn't notice much.
   d. pays close attention.

10. One **glory** of nature is a
    a. muggy night.
    b. lovely sunset.
    c. dust storm.
    d. mosquito bite.

Definitions Study the spelling, pronunciation, part of speech, and definition for each word. Write the word on the line in the sentence. Then read the synonyms and antonyms.

1. **audible**
('ô də bəl)

(adj.) capable of being heard

The music was _____ down the street.

SYNONYMS: loud, clear, distinct; ANTONYMS: inaudible, faint, indistinct

2. **consume**
(kən 'süm)

(v.) to eat or drink, especially in large amounts; to use up; to destroy

We plan to _____ an early dinner.

SYNONYMS: devour; waste, deplete; destroy, demolish, annihilate, vanquish

3. **glide**
(glīd)

(v.) to move smoothly and easily

I watched the airplane _____ through the sky.

SYNONYMS: slide, coast, cruise, sail

4. **origin**
('ôr ə jən)

(n.) the cause or beginning

The _____ of chocolate is the cacao tree.

SYNONYMS: beginning, start, source, root, parentage, ancestry, lineage
ANTONYMS: end, finish, death, demise

5. **prevent**
(pri 'vent)

(v.) to stop from happening

Waterproof boots _____ feet from getting wet.

SYNONYMS: bar, block, prohibit, hamper, hinder, restrain, obstruct
ANTONYMS: allow, permit, encourage

6. **punctuate**
(pənk chū 'wāt)

(v.) to mark printed or written materials with periods, commas, and other signs; to interrupt from time to time; to give importance to

I was careful in how I chose to _____ my writing.

SYNONYMS: interrupt; emphasize, accentuate

A speed skater **glides** (word 3) to a medal in the Olympics.

7. **representative**
(rep ri 'zen tə tiv)

(n.) a typical example; someone who acts for another

She was the company's _____ *at the meeting.*

(adj.) having to do with elected members; being a typical example

That painting is _____ *of modern art.*

SYNONYMS: (n.) example, type, specimen, agent, spokesperson, delegate, ambassador; (adj.) elected, chosen; typical, characteristic, illustrative
ANTONYMS: (adj.) atypical, unrepresentative

8. **scorn**
(skôrn)

(n.) a feeling that something or someone is worthless or inferior; an expression of that feeling

It is not right to treat those who are less fortunate with _____.

(v.) to act with contempt toward an object or a person; to make fun of

I wish they did not _____ *my old bicycle.*

SYNONYMS: (n. & v.) ridicule, disdain; (n.) contempt, disrespect, mockery, derision; (v.) mock, dismiss, reject, spurn, scoff, sneer
ANTONYMS: (n.) admiration, praise; (v.) approve, embrace

9. **stout**
(staut)

(adj.) large and heavy in build; physically strong and sturdy; having courage or determination

The _____ *old maples survived the wind storms.*

SYNONYMS: brave, bold, courageous, forceful; sturdy, vigorous; fat, heavy
ANTONYMS: cowardly, timid; infirm, weak; thin

10. **woe**
(wō)

(n.) great sorrow or suffering; trouble

I felt such _____ *when my poor dog died.*

SYNONYMS: sadness, unhappiness, misery, sorrow, grief, despondency; misfortune, suffering; ANTONYMS: happiness, joy; luck

Choose the word whose meaning is suggested by the clue given. Then write the word on the line provided.

1. To _____ is to emphasize.
   a. consume   b. glide   c. punctuate

2. When people feel _____, they feel sadness.
   a. representative   b. scorn   c. woe

3. If you _____ something, you use it up.
   a. glide   b. consume   c. prevent

4. The source of a story is its _____.
   a. woe   b. origin   c. representative

5. When a sound can be heard, it is _____.
   a. audible   b. representative   c. stout

6. To _____ is to move along without much effort.
   a. consume   b. punctuate   c. glide

7. When you sneer at something, you show _____ for it.
   a. origin   b. woe   c. scorn

8. If you try to _____ something, you are trying to stop it from happening.
   a. prevent   b. consume   c. glide

9. Something that is _____ might also be called sturdy.
   a. audible   b. representative   c. stout

10. A(n) _____ statement can be a typical one.
    a. audible   b. representative   c. stout

Synonyms *Choose the word that is most nearly the **same** in meaning as the word or phrase in **dark print**. Then write your choice on the line provided.*

1. the **root** of their unhappiness
   a. scorn   b. woe   c. origin   _____

2. **cruise** along peacefully
   a. consume   b. prevent   c. glide   _____

3. **emphasize** my remarks
   a. glide   b. prevent   c. punctuate   _____

4. showed terrible **disrespect**
   a. scorn   b. origin   c. woe   _____

5. a **loud** screech
   a. audible   b. stout   c. representative _____

6. **deplete** your energy
   a. scorn   b. consume   c. glide   _____

Antonyms *Choose the word that is most nearly the **opposite** in meaning to the word or phrase in **dark print**. Then write your choice on the line provided.*

1. was overcome with **joy**
   a. scorn   b. origin   c. woe   _____

2. an **atypical** example
   a. audible   b. stout   c. representative _____

3. a **cowardly** heart
   a. stout   b. audible   c. representative _____

4. **allow** the discussion
   a. prevent   b. consume   c. punctuate   _____

From the list of words on pages 82–83, choose the one that best completes each item below. Then write the word on the line provided. (You may have to change the word's ending.)

Astronauts in Space

Astronauts looking down on Earth from space can see oceans and land, but no sounds are _____ from our planet.

In a spaceship, the astronauts' bodies _____ around smoothly because there is no gravity pulling them down.

Astronauts must _____ their food from freeze-dried packets.

Even though this food is not very tasty, astronauts must eat in order to _____ weakness.

Opera

The _____ of the term *opera* is the Italian phrase *opera in musica*, meaning "work in music."

There are many styles of opera. Therefore, we cannot say that any one opera is _____ of the musical form.

People used to think that opera singers needed to have bodies that are _____ and sturdy. However, many opera singers who have powerful voices are actually quite thin.

Many operas deal with touching human stories. Often, a character feels _____ by a loved one. This situation leads to songs that show strong feelings of _____.

Moments of great drama can be _____ by trumpets blaring.

Word Associations

*Circle the letter next to the choice that best completes the sentence or answers the question. Pay special attention to the word in **dark print**.*

1. You can **glide** on floors that
   a. have thick carpeting.
   b. are bumpy.
   c. are broken and have splints.
   d. are shiny and polished.

2. A healthy cow will **consume**
   a. a lot of grass.
   b. gallons of milk.
   c. sides of beef.
   d. strips of leather.

3. The **origin** of a river is
   a. how deep it is.
   b. how fast its water moves.
   c. where it begins to flow.
   d. who swims in it.

4. If you feel **scorn** for someone, you might show it by
   a. flashing a big smile.
   b. giving a mean look.
   c. taking a photograph.
   d. inviting the person to dinner.

5. Expect a **stout** soldier to be
   a. short and skinny.
   b. funny and smart.
   c. brave and strong.
   d. weak and timid.

6. Which knows if something is **audible**?
   a. the tongue
   b. the nose
   c. the eyes
   d. the ears

7. How do you **prevent** hunger?
   a. Provide enough food.
   b. Go on a diet.
   c. Hide all the food.
   d. Eat only vegetables.

8. You might **punctuate** a sentence
   a. with a hammer.
   b. with a question mark.
   c. with an eraser.
   d. with a paragraph.

9. A **representative** on the student council has the power to
   a. plan everyone's vacation.
   b. lift weights.
   c. vote on school issues.
   d. win a spelling bee.

10. Which shows a feeling of **woe**?
   a. "Oh, what a treat!"
   b. "Oh, I don't mind."
   c. "Oh, we think so!"
   d. "Oh, how terrible!"

Definitions *Study the spelling, pronunciation, part of speech, and definition for each word. Write the word on the line in the sentence. Then read the synonyms and antonyms.*

1. **arch**
   (arch)

   (n.) a curved structure that serves as an opening and as a support

   The door to the castle had an _____ over it.

   (v.) to form a curve

   The puppeteer attempted to _____ the puppet's eyebrows.

   (adj.) main; playful, mischievous

   We jokingly called the opposing team our _____ enemies.

   SYNONYMS: (n. & v.) curve; (n.) archway, curvature, semicircle; (adj.) chief, principal; playful, mischievous, sly
   ANTONYMS: (adj.) minor, lesser, secondary

2. **authentic**
   (ô 'then tik)

   (adj.) being the real thing; worthy of belief, true

   That is an _____ diamond necklace.

   SYNONYMS: real, actual, true, genuine, sincere
   ANTONYMS: fake, false, counterfeit, inauthentic

3. **clarify**
   ('klar ə fī)

   (v.) to say clearly or make easier to understand

   The teacher tried to _____ the assignment.

   SYNONYMS: explain, simplify, illuminate, demystify
   ANTONYMS: bewilder, complicate, mystify, obscure, perplex, puzzle

4. **declare**
   (di 'klâr)

   (v.) to state strongly; to make a formal or an official statement

   I was too shy to _____ my feelings.

   SYNONYMS: state, affirm, announce, assert, proclaim
   ANTONYM: deny

5. **grant**
   (grant)

   (v.) to permit or allow; to admit that something is true

   The leader decided to _____ their request.

   (n.) something that is given

   They received a _____ to study other cultures.

   SYNONYMS: (v. & n.) award; (v.) bequeath, bestow, accord; admit, allow, acknowledge, concede; (n.) gift, present, endowment
   ANTONYMS: (v.) refuse, disallow, rescind

In the sport of fencing, **opponents** (word 8) challenge each other with a special kind of sword.

6. **grave**
   (grāv)

   (n.) a hole in the ground where something is buried

   The _____ of President Ulysses S. Grant is in New York City.

   (adj.) very important and requiring much attention; serious, solemn

   The climbers were in _____ danger.

   SYNONYMS: (n.) tomb, sepulcher; (adj.) critical, significant; sober, solemn, somber, subdued
   ANTONYMS: (adj.) cheerful, joking, light, lighthearted, merry, sunny, frivolous; insignificant, unimportant

7. **modest**
   ('mä dəst)

   (adj.) not thinking too highly of oneself, not boastful; proper in speech, dress, or behavior; not extreme or large, moderate

   We were surprised at how _____ the famous singer was.

   SYNONYMS: reserved, proper, humble, shy, diffident; simple, chaste, demure; moderate, unpretentious
   ANTONYMS: bold, conceited, proud, self-assured, vain; flamboyant; excessive, grand, imposing

8. **opponent**
   (ə 'pō nənt)

   (n.) someone who is set against another, as in a contest, game, argument, or fight

   My _____ in the chess match beat me in the first round.

   SYNONYMS: foe, rival, enemy, competitor, challenger, antagonist
   ANTONYMS: ally, partner, colleague, helper, friend, teammate

9. **valid**
   ('va ləd)

   (adj.) supported by facts or evidence, true

   Your report presents many _____ arguments.

   SYNONYMS: true, cogent, convincing, justifiable, persuasive, sound
   ANTONYMS: dubious, false, invalid, unconvincing

10. **yearn**
    (yərn)

    (v.) to long for

    I _____ for our vacation.

    SYNONYMS: desire, wish, want, crave, need, pine, hunger, thirst

Choose the word whose meaning is suggested by the clue given. Then write the word on the line provided.

1. The person you are playing against is your _____.
   a. arch   b. opponent   c. grave

2. To want something very much is to _____ for it.
   a. yearn   b. clarify   c. declare

3. An object that is _____ is real and not a copy.
   a. grave   b. authentic   c. modest

4. When you make a strong statement, you _____ something.
   a. declare   b. arch   c. grant

5. Their faces may look _____ if they're arguing.
   a. modest   b. valid   c. grave

6. To permit something to happen is to _____ it.
   a. clarify   b. yearn   c. grant

7. A(n) _____ has a curved shape.
   a. opponent   b. grave   c. arch

8. When you _____ what you say, you make it easy to understand.
   a. declare   b. clarify   c. grant

9. A(n) _____ argument is said to be true and correct.
   a. valid   b. modest   c. arch

10. A(n) _____ amount is a small amount.
    a. authentic   b. grave   c. modest

Synonyms

*Choose the word that is most nearly the **same** in meaning as the word or phrase in **dark print**. Then write your choice on the line provided.*

1. a frightening **foe**
   a. grant   b. arch   c. opponent   _____

2. **pine** for a banana
   a. clarify   b. yearn   c. declare   _____

3. a **solemn** event
   a. grave   b. arch   c. valid   _____

4. **announce** the winner
   a. yearn   b. clarify   c. declare   _____

5. **concede** the favor
   a. grant   b. arch   c. clarify   _____

6. a **mischievous** smile
   a. authentic   b. modest   c. arch   _____

Antonyms

*Choose the word that is most nearly the **opposite** in meaning to the word or phrase in **dark print**. Then write your choice on the line provided.*

1. **fake** coins
   a. arch   b. authentic   c. modest   _____

2. an **invalid** winner
   a. modest   b. valid   c. grave   _____

3. a **vain** gymnast
   a. valid   b. authentic   c. modest   _____

4. **complicate** the math lesson
   a. clarify   b. declare   c. yearn   _____

Completing the Sentence

From the list of words on pages 88–89, choose the one that best completes each item below. Then write the word on the line provided. (You may have to change the word's ending.)

Baseball

Part of the job of a baseball announcer is to _____ the names of the players and the score.

A good announcer will also try to _____ the complicated rules of the game.

It's always nice to find major league players who are _____ and do not like to brag about themselves.

All players _____ to play a good game. Of course, what they want above all else is to beat their _____.

That is certainly a _____ goal, but no team can win all the time, no matter how hard it tries.

Museums

We saw designs of Greek temples in the museum and learned that the _____ above the doorways can have a point at the top.

We also learned that the paintings in the museum are not fakes but _____.

Many museums offer _____ to students, which allow them to study how the artworks were made.

Some students even dig up old _____ in ancient cities to learn about people who lived in the past.

Word Associations

*Circle the letter next to the choice that best completes the sentence or answers the question. Pay special attention to the word in **dark print**.*

1. You need to **clarify** rules that
   a. are easy to follow.
   b. are not important.
   c. are complicated.
   d. nobody cares about.

2. People usually have **grave** looks on their faces when they are
   a. at a circus.
   b. at a funeral.
   c. at a brunch.
   d. at a party.

3. Your **opponent** probably wants
   a. to help you.
   b. to feed you.
   c. to lose to you.
   d. to beat you.

4. Which forms a natural **arch**?
   a. a horseshoe
   b. an octopus
   c. a monkey
   d. a brick

5. A **valid** fishing license
   a. is no longer legal.
   b. is impossible to get.
   c. is in effect now.
   d. says that fish are real.

6. An **authentic** Japanese coin
   a. is not real.
   b. comes from Japan.
   c. is made in America.
   d. can be used in America.

7. What might you say when you **grant** my request?
   a. "You may have your wish."
   b. "I won't ever agree to it."
   c. "That is not allowed."
   d. "I will never do anything for you."

8. An actor might **yearn** most for
   a. an old costume.
   b. a leading role.
   c. a broken leg.
   d. a bad performance.

9. A **modest** piece of cake would be
   a. huge.
   b. salty.
   c. small.
   d. chocolate.

10. You **declare** something if you
    a. are just waking up.
    b. are in the middle of a deep sleep.
    c. feel unsure about that thing.
    d. feel strongly about that thing.

Definitions *Study the spelling, pronunciation, part of speech, and definition for each word. Write the word on the line in the sentence. Then read the synonyms and antonyms.*

1. **admirable**
   ('ad mə rə bəl)

   (adj.) deserving praise

   The murals they painted on the wall are _____.

   SYNONYMS: excellent, superior, wonderful, praiseworthy, first-rate
   ANTONYMS: inferior, mediocre, second-rate

2. **automatic**
   (ô tə 'ma tik)

   (adj.) done without thought or will; done by a machine, not by a human

   Blinking is an _____ response.

   SYNONYMS: involuntary, instinctive, unconscious, mechanical
   ANTONYMS: deliberate, conscious, voluntary, intentional

3. **devotion**
   (di 'vō shən)

   (n.) loyalty and affection

   They showed their _____ to their religious faith by attending services on a regular basis.

   SYNONYMS: attachment, commitment, dedication, faith, loyalty, allegiance
   ANTONYMS: disloyalty, faithlessness, infidelity

4. **distant**
   ('dis tənt)

   (adj.) far away; not friendly

   The _____ cabin was difficult to get to.

   SYNONYMS: far, remote, apart, removed, separated; reserved, unapproachable, aloof, unfriendly, detached, cold
   ANTONYMS: near, close, adjacent, neighboring; accessible, affable, warm

5. **dreary**
   ('drir ē)

   (adj.) gloomy or dismal; without cheer, comfort, or enthusiasm

   The rain did not stop at all during the _____ afternoon.

   SYNONYMS: gloomy, depressing, bleak, dismal, languid, listless, sluggish
   ANTONYMS: cheery, exciting, vibrant, lively, merry

6. **exhaust**
   (ig 'zôst)

   (v.) to use up; to wear out

   Try not to _____ all your energy shopping at the mall.

Harry Houdini, the great magician and escape artist, thrilled the world by performing many original and dangerous **stunts** (word 10).

(n.) the escape of gas from an engine

The _____ from the bus made me choke.

SYNONYMS: (v.) tire, fatigue, weaken, consume, deplete, drain, empty
ANTONYMS: (v.) animate, enliven, fill, invigorate, quicken

7. **kindle**
('kin dəl)

(v.) to get a fire going; to stir up or to start something

We tried to _____ a campfire.

SYNONYMS: ignite, burn, fuel, light; arouse, awaken, excite, rouse, stimulate
ANTONYMS: discourage, dampen, stifle, extinguish, deaden

8. **predict**
(pri 'dikt)

(v.) to guess what is going to happen

It is difficult to _____ what will occur tomorrow.

SYNONYMS: forecast, foretell, foresee, anticipate, expect, guess

9. **separation**
(se pə rā shən)

(n.) the act or condition of being apart

They met again after a _____ of ten years.

SYNONYMS: disconnection, detachment, rift, break, division, isolation
ANTONYMS: connection, attachment, unification, integration, continuity

10. **stunt**
(stənt)

(v.) to stop or slow down the growth of

The scientist worked to _____ the growth of the weed.

(n.) an act that shows great strength, bravery, or skill, often to get attention

The circus is a perfect place to try out a daring _____.

SYNONYMS: (v.) block, hamper, hinder, impede, curtail, suppress, restrain, obstruct; (n.) feat, performance, achievement, exploit
ANTONYMS: (v.) encourage, stimulate, propel

 **Match the Meaning**

Choose the word whose meaning is suggested by the clue given. Then write the word on the line provided.

1. To _____ is to make a guess about what will happen.
   a. kindle   b. stunt   c. predict

2. Something _____ might be described as excellent.
   a. automatic   b. distant   c. admirable

3. A feat that displays much skill is a(n) _____.
   a. exhaust   b. stunt   c. devotion

4. To be far apart is to be _____.
   a. admirable   b. automatic   c. distant

5. A(n) _____ reaction is one that happens without thought.
   a. admirable   b. dreary   c. automatic

6. To show _____ is to show loyalty.
   a. devotion   b. separation   c. stunt

7. A(n) _____ from people might also be a detachment from them.
   a. exhaust   b. devotion   c. separation

8. A(n) _____ afternoon can also be considered gloomy.
   a. distant   b. dreary   c. automatic

9. To light a fire is to _____ it.
   a. predict   b. kindle   c. stunt

10. The fumes that come from an engine are called _____.
    a. separation   b. material   c. exhaust

Synonyms

*Choose the word that is most nearly the **same** in meaning as the word or phrase in **dark print.** Then write your choice on the line provided.*

1. **tire out** the workers
   a. exhaust   b. kindle   c. predict   _____

2. **forecast** the weather
   a. kindle   b. exhaust   c. predict   _____

3. **hamper** your progress
   a. kindle   b. exhaust   c. stunt   _____

4. an **excellent** way with animals
   a. automatic   b. admirable   c. distant   _____

5. an **involuntary** thought
   a. automatic   b. admirable   c. dreary   _____

Antonyms

*Choose the word that is most nearly the **opposite** in meaning to the word or phrase in **dark print.** Then write your choice on the line provided.*

1. a painful **attachment**
   a. devotion   b. separation   c. stunt   _____

2. a **cheery** scene
   a. admirable   b. automatic   c. dreary   _____

3. **extinguish** the flame
   a. kindle   b. stunt   c. exhaust   _____

4. a soldier's **disloyalty**
   a. stunt   b. separation   c. devotion   _____

5. a **close** relative
   a. admirable   b. distant   c. automatic   _____

Completing the Sentence

From the list of words on pages 94–95, choose the one that best completes each item below. Then write the word on the line provided. (You may have to change the word's ending.)

Winter

Many people find the long, cold winter to be _____.

It helps the mood to _____ a fire and warm up by the fireplace.

Winter sports can also help a person's frame of mind. It can be fun to ice skate for hours, even if it _____ you!

Sometimes, however, the winter seems as if it will never end. Spring seems to be a _____ dream.

My Friend, the Gardener

I have a friend who is an _____ gardener. Everything he plants grows beautifully.

The _____ he shows to every detail of his garden is impressive.

He's always happy when the weather forecasters _____ rain. That is because he knows that if it doesn't rain, the plants' growth will be _____ by lack of water.

When he goes away, he turns on an _____ sprinkler that will water his garden in his absence.

If you want my friend to be happy, make sure there is never too long a _____ between him and his garden!

Word Associations

*Circle the letter next to the choice that best completes the sentence or answers the question. Pay special attention to the word in **dark print**.*

1. To show **devotion** to learning,
   a. come late to class.
   b. do your homework.
   c. forget to study.
   d. skip school.

2. If you seem **distant** to someone,
   a. you are warm.
   b. you are cold.
   c. you are friendly.
   d. you are happy.

3. You might see physical **stunts** at the
   a. computer.
   b. hardware store.
   c. grocery store.
   d. circus.

4. If you feel **exhausted**, you might
   a. jog a few miles.
   b. paint a picture.
   c. take a nap.
   d. learn to skate.

5. A long **separation** would be
   a. a lot of time to wait.
   b. a little time to wait.
   c. something to look forward to.
   d. something you probably wouldn't notice.

6. It's an **admirable** trait to be
   a. polite.
   b. grumpy.
   c. selfish.
   d. boring.

7. On a dark and **dreary** Saturday afternoon, you might feel
   a. encouraged
   b. discouraged.
   c. honored.
   d. hopeful.

8. You can **predict** the score for
   a. last night's ballgame.
   b. yesterday's ballgame.
   c. tomorrow's ballgame.
   d. last week's ballgame.

9. Which is best to **kindle** a fire?
   a. water
   b. soda
   c. plastic
   d. matches

10. Which of the following is done **automatically**?
    a. driving
    b. eating
    c. drinking
    d. breathing

Selecting Word Meanings

*Circle the choice that is most nearly the **same** in meaning as the word in **dark print**.*

1. under our **watchful** eyes
   a. blue   b. observant   c. sleepy   d. shining

2. **glide** through the test
   a. sail   b. stumble   c. struggle   d. sing

3. near a stone **arch**
   a. chair   b. table   c. path   d. curve

4. a **separation** of items
   a. listing   b. selling   c. division   d. addition

5. painted it a **dreary** color
   a. cheerful   b. gentle   c. gloomy   d. calming

6. learning a new **stunt**
   a. act   b. song   c. recipe   d. prayer

7. as we **approach** the cabin
   a. build   b. describe   c. clean   d. near

8. was **audible** for hours
   a. asleep   b. quiet   c. patient   d. loud

9. gave us a large **grant**
   a. meal   b. gift   c. piece   d. assignment

10. a **valid** reason
    a. strange   b. possible   c. convincing   d. weak

Spelling

*Study the word in **dark print**. If a letter is missing, fill in the blank to make a correctly spelled word. If the word is already spelled correctly, leave the blank empty.*

1. **ap__rove** the project

2. a Mexican **tr__dition**

3. **punc__uate** clearly

4. a **representativ__** action

5. an **aut__entic** battle sword

6. a **m__dest** walk

7. **automa__ic** writing

8. **ex__aust** the supplies

9. gave a **prom__t** answer

10. **con__sume** the whole thing

Antonyms

*Circle the choice that is most nearly the **opposite** in meaning as the word in **dark print**.*

1. **revive** the play
   a. repeat   b. perform   c. kill   d. edit

2. the **origin** of that plan
   a. demise   b. source   c. follower   d. surprise

3. **declare** their interest
   a. announce   b. believe   c. ignore   d. deny

4. gave **admirable** advice
   a. excellent   b. inferior   c. sensible   d. painful

5. showed his true **devotion**
   a. faith   b. colors   c. disloyalty   d. ability

Vocabulary in Context

Words have been left out of the following passage. For each numbered item in the passage, fill in the circle next to the word in the margin that best fills the blank space.

Do you know the sad tale of the *Titanic*? The *Titanic* was a __1__ ocean liner. It had all the modern features of its day. It was grand and fast. And it was huge! People called it the safest ship ever built. It was thought to be "unsinkable." No one could __2__ what would happen on the *Titanic's* very first voyage.

Before airplanes, traveling by ship was the only way to cross the oceans. Crossing the Atlantic Ocean took at least a week to do back then. Eager travelers __3__ for a spot on the new *Titanic*. They looked forward to a speedy and thrilling trip.

The *Titanic* left England on April 10, 1912. More than 2,200 passengers and crew members were on board. People felt joyful. There were big parties as the ship sailed. Everybody expected a fine, smooth, and safe trip. But that was not to be.

A little before midnight five days later, the *Titanic* hit an iceberg. Nobody knew at first how bad the damage was. People were very calm. But soon it was clear that the ship was doomed. Crew members tried to __4__ panic. They saved as many lives as they could. In less than three hours, the *Titanic* had split into two pieces. It sank into the deep, cold sea.

More than 700 people got into lifeboats. Those lucky ones were rescued and brought safely to New York. But more than 1,500 people were lost. The __5__ came to rest on the ocean floor. The remains of the *Titanic* still rest there today.

1. ○ small
   ○ regular
   ○ magnificent
   ○ simple

2. ○ consume
   ○ predict
   ○ approach
   ○ remember

3. ○ yearned
   ○ yawned
   ○ exhausted
   ○ revived

4. ○ approve
   ○ declare
   ○ allow
   ○ prevent

5. ○ signal
   ○ opponent
   ○ wreckage
   ○ stunt

Analogies

Circle the item that best completes the comparison. Then explain the relationship on the lines provided.

1. **bold** is to **meek** as
   a. stout is to slim
   b. dreary is to dull
   c. strong is to tough
   d. look is to peek

   Relationship: _____

   _____

   _____

2. **approve** is to **admire** as
   a. leave is to stay
   b. kindle is to fire
   c. woe is to representative
   d. scorn is to dismiss

   Relationship: _____

   _____

   _____

   _____

3. **ear** is to **audible** as
   a. peace is to possible
   b. eye is to visible
   c. nose is to terrible
   d. hair is to likeable

   Relationship: _____

   _____

   _____

4. **opponent** is to **enemy** as
   a. rival is to friend
   b. opposite is to same
   c. partner is to helper
   d. war is to peace

   Relationship: _____

   _____

   _____

Challenge: Make up your own

Write a comparison using the words in the box. Then explain the relationship on the lines provided.

authentic	refuse	grant	false

Analogy: _____ is to _____ as _____ is to _____ .

Relationship: _____

_____

Word Families

*The words in **dark print** in the sentences below are related to words introduced in Units 9–12. For example, the adjectives predictable and traditional in Item 1 are related to the verb predict (Unit 12) and the noun tradition (Unit 9). Circle the related word in **dark print** that best completes each sentence.*

approach	clarify	grave	modest	prompt
approve	consume	kindle	origin	scorn
authentic	distant	magnificent	predict	tradition
automatic	glory	meek	prevent	valid

1. The weather is always so **(predictable/traditional)** in Hawaii.

2. The city passes laws to protect the **(approval/consumer)**.

3. The **(original/glorious)** Grand Canyon is a popular tourist spot.

4. This remote control **(automatically/modestly)** opens our garage door.

5. Scientists can test the **(authenticity/distance)** of old artworks.

6. What can you do to help in the **(prevention/promptness)** of pollution?

7. We can use newspapers as **(clarification/kindling)** for the bonfire.

8. Loud music and dancing does not fit the **(gravity/validity)** of this occasion.

9. That **(approachable/scornful)** remark hurt my feelings.

10. The **(magnificence/meekness)** of the grand palace is proper for a royal family.

Use the clues below to complete the crossword puzzle.
(All of the answers are words from Units 9–12.)

Across

1. ruins after an accident
5. deeply long for something
8. someone who is against you in a contest
9. [image]

Down

2. bring back to life
3. honor, praise, or greatness
4. to make something easy to understand
6. waste gas that comes out of an engine
7. to state with strong feeling
8. the beginning of something
10. a feeling that someone is inferior

11. dismal, gloomy, or sluggish
12. to slow down normal growth
13. to stir up or start something

Definitions *Study the spelling, pronunciation, part of speech, and definition for each word. Write the word on the line in the sentence. Then read the synonyms and antonyms.*

1. **abundant**
   (ə 'bun dənt)

   (adj.) large or more than enough; plentiful

   There was an _____ amount of food at the restaurant.

   SYNONYMS: plentiful, profuse, copious, bountiful
   ANTONYMS: deficient, meager, scant, sparse, scarce

2. **barrier**
   ('bar ē ər)

   (n.) something that blocks or bars movement or passage

   The mountains acted as a _____ to the wind.

   SYNONYMS: wall, obstacle, barricade, roadblock, deterrent, impediment, obstruction, restraint
   ANTONYMS: entrance, passageway

3. **conceive**
   (kən 'sēv)

   (v.) to start something; to think up or begin to understand

   I began to _____ a plan on how to get all my work done.

   SYNONYMS: form, formulate, develop, devise, imagine, think, understand

4. **formal**
   ('fôr məl)

   (adj.) following strict rules or customs; requiring fancy clothes and fine manners

   The club members were required to follow a _____ dress code.

   SYNONYMS: official, conventional, standard; ceremonial; proper, fancy
   ANTONYMS: informal, unofficial, casual

5. **inquire**
   (in 'kwīr)

   (v.) to ask about

   The detective has begun to _____ about the crime.

   SYNONYMS: ask, investigate, query, question, quiz, probe, examine, explore, interrogate, study
   ANTONYMS: answer, reply, respond, retort

A cat finds a bathtub a comfortable place to **slumber** (word 10).

6. **penalize**
('pē nəl īz)

(v.) to punish

Our teacher will _____ us for talking out of turn.

SYNONYMS: discipline, punish, castigate, chasten
ANTONYM: reward

7. **picturesque**
(pik chə 'resk)

(adj.) charming, quaint

The little town is _____.

SYNONYMS: beautiful, pretty, lovely, striking, vivid, scenic, quaint, delightful
ANTONYMS: ugly, drab, dull, grim, unpleasant, distasteful

8. **predator**
('pre də tər)

(n.) one that destroys or devours others; an animal that stalks and eats other animals

Snakes are _____ of mice and other rodents.

SYNONYMS: thief, bandit, looter, pilferer, pillager, plunderer, poacher

9. **privilege**
('priv lij)

(n.) a special right, benefit, or permission

The players who arrived first got the _____ of choosing the nicest uniforms.

SYNONYMS: right, benefit, advantage, honor, prerogative

10. **slumber**
('sləm bər)

(v.) to sleep lightly

The baby will _____ for a while after lunch.

(n.) a sleep or light sleep

The cat lay in a _____ for most of the afternoon.

SYNONYMS: (v. & n.) sleep, nap, doze, rest, snooze, repose
ANTONYMS: (v.) awake, arouse, stir; (n.) awareness

 **Match the Meaning**

Choose the word whose meaning is suggested by the clue given. Then write the word on the line provided.

1. A _____ blocks the way or does not allow passage.
   a. barrier   b. privilege   c. slumber

2. To _____ is to give a punishment or penalty.
   a. conceive   b. slumber   c. penalize

3. An invitation to a(n) _____ party might request that you dress in a fancy way.
   a. formal   b. abundant   c. picturesque

4. If you fall asleep, you are said to _____.
   a. penalize   b. inquire   c. slumber

5. To think of a plan or an idea is to _____ it.
   a. inquire   b. conceive   c. penalize

6. A _____ is known to attack and eat its prey.
   a. barrier   b. privilege   c. predator

7. When you _____ about a story, you ask about it.
   a. inquire   b. slumber   c. conceive

8. An amount that is _____ is a large amount.
   a. formal   b. abundant   c. picturesque

9. An advantage or right can also be known as a _____.
   a. predator   b. barrier   c. privilege

10. The colorful scene was described to the artists as _____.
    a. formal   b. abundant   c. picturesque

Synonyms

*Choose the word that is most nearly the **same** in meaning as the word or phrase in **dark print**. Then write your choice on the line provided.*

1. a nasty **bandit**
   a. privilege   b. predator   c. barrier   _____

2. the **right** to leave
   a. predator   b. privilege   c. slumber   _____

3. a huge **obstacle**
   a. barrier   b. predator   c. privilege   _____

4. **discipline** the naughty dog
   a. conceive   b. inquire   c. penalize   _____

5. **think of** a clever idea
   a. conceive   b. penalize   c. slumber   _____

Antonyms

*Choose the word that is most nearly the **opposite** in meaning to the word or phrase in **dark print**. Then write your choice on the line provided.*

1. caused me to **awake**
   a. penalize   b. inquire   c. slumber   _____

2. a **drab** city
   a. formal   b. abundant   c. picturesque   _____

3. the **meager** number of birthday cards
   a. formal   b. abundant   c. picturesque   _____

4. **reply** right away
   a. penalize   b. slumber   c. inquire   _____

5. a **casual** hello
   a. abundant   b. formal   c. picturesque   _____

From the list of words on pages 106–107, choose the one that best completes each item below. Then write the word on the line provided. (You may have to change the word's ending.)

Etymology

When we study the history of a word, or its etymology, we learn of its beginnings and how it has come to be a part of our language.

The word _____, which we use to describe something that bars the way, comes from the French word *barre*. Dancers use a barre to stretch their legs.

A pretty scene is _____. This word comes from *pictor*, the Latin word for painter.

Many English words are the result of the joining of two or more Latin words. For example, _____ comes from *privus*, the word for "private" and *lex*, the word for "law."

The English word _____, which means "to ask about," comes from the Latin word *quaerere*, which means "to seek."

Both the English word _____ and its ancient relative *praedator*, come from the Latin word which means "to seize or capture."

Skiing

I went skiing last week. There was a blizzard the night before, which left a(n) _____ amount of snow.

It was hard to _____ how I would make it all the way down the tall mountain without falling!

Since that was hard to imagine, I decided to try an easier slope at a lower level. No one would _____ me for being cautious.

Some ski outfits were so fancy that they made skiing seem as if it were a _____ sport!

At the end of the day we fell into a peaceful _____ by the fire.

Word Associations

*Circle the letter next to the choice that best completes the sentence or answers the question. Pay special attention to the word in **dark print**.*

1. If you **conceive** a plan, you are
   a. the last one to know about it.
   b. the first to think of it.
   c. the only one who supports it.
   d. not interested in it.

2. Visit a **picturesque** town to see its
   a. big parking lots.
   b. smelly trash dump.
   c. modern gas stations.
   d. charming old houses.

3. When you **slumber**, you might
   a. have a dream.
   b. read a book.
   c. ride a bike.
   d. knit a scarf.

4. An **abundant** amount of fruit is
   a. against the law.
   b. a little bit of fruit.
   c. a lot of fruit.
   d. no fruit at all.

5. A **formal** greeting is
   a. "How do you do?"
   b. "Hey, dude!"
   c. "Howdy, pal."
   d. "See you later, alligator."

6. With which would you **inquire**?
   a. "Let me take your coat."
   b. "This is my ID card."
   c. "May I ask a question?"
   d. "I would love to help."

7. A library might **penalize** you if you
   a. damage one of its books.
   b. love to read.
   c. use the encyclopedia.
   d. live nearby.

8. Which is a **predator** of chickens?
   a. an egg
   b. a fox
   c. a turkey
   d. a mouse

9. Which **privilege** do you think most kids would choose?
   a. to do four hours of homework
   b. to eat spinach and liver
   c. to scrub the bathroom floor
   d. to stay up as late as they want

10. The hiker turns back at a **barrier**
    a. made out of dust.
    b. made with a map.
    c. made by a fallen tree.
    d. made of whipped cream.

Definitions *Study the spelling, pronunciation, part of speech, and definition for each word. Write the word on the line in the sentence. Then read the synonyms and antonyms.*

1. **advantage**
   (əd 'van tij)

   (n.) something that puts someone in a better position

   The _____ of sitting up front is being able to see the movie better.

   SYNONYMS: benefit, gain, edge, asset
   ANTONYMS: disadvantage, detriment, drawback, handicap

2. **ambition**
   (am 'bi shən)

   (n.) a strong desire for importance or success

   My _____ is to be an excellent artist.

   SYNONYMS: aim, aspiration, goal

3. **defiant**
   (di 'fī ənt)

   (adj.) showing strong resistance; willing to challenge or confront

   The _____ team member refused to listen to the coach.

   SYNONYMS: rebellious, disobedient, insubordinant, noncompliant; bold
   ANTONYMS: submissive, yielding

4. **fearsome**
   ('fir səm)

   (adj.) frightening or alarming

   That horror movie was quite _____.

   SYNONYMS: scary, frightening, alarming, terrifying, horrifying
   ANTONYMS: reassuring, comforting, encouraging

5. **imply**
   (im 'plī)

   (v.) to suggest something without saying it directly

   Their kind remarks _____ that they want me to join in.

   SYNONYMS: hint, indicate, suggest
   ANTONYMS: declare, state, announce

World leaders sometimes meet to **negotiate** (word 7) agreements. Here President Ronald Reagan and Soviet leader Mikhail Gorbachev shake hands after signing an arms control agreement in 1987.

6. **merit**
   ('mer ət)

   (n.) a quality that deserves praise

   The chief _____ of the book is its surprise ending.

   (v.) to be worthy of, deserve

   We _____ good grades for our hard work.

   SYNONYMS: (n.) value, virtue, worth, excellence, achievement;
   (v.) deserve, earn, warrant
   ANTONYMS: (n.) inferiority, fault

7. **negotiate**
   (ni 'gō shē āt)

   (v.) to discuss in order to arrive at an agreement

   Professional athletes usually have agents who _____ their contracts.

   SYNONYMS: discuss, debate

8. **purify**
   ('pyur ə fī)

   (v.) to make clean and free of dirt or pollutants

   We need to _____ the dirty water so we can drink it.

   SYNONYMS: clean, cleanse, filter, freshen, refine, sanitize
   ANTONYMS: pollute, contaminate, cloud, dirty, muddy, soil

9. **revoke**
   (ri 'vōk)

   (v.) to cancel by withdrawing or reversing

   The judge decided to _____ his license.

   SYNONYMS: annul, cancel, remove, repeal, rescind
   ANTONYMS: give, offer, provide, supply

10. **wretched**
    ('re chəd)

    (adj.) very unhappy or unfortunate, miserable; very poor in quality

    We felt _____ about the terrible accident.

    SYNONYMS: depressed, miserable, dejected, unfortunate, inferior, dreadful
    ANTONYMS: happy, pleased, elated, great, superior

Choose the word whose meaning is suggested by the clue given. Then write the word on the line provided.

1. To refuse to obey authority is to be _____.
   a. defiant   b. wretched   c. fearsome

2. To have a(n) _____ is to be in a better position than others are.
   a. ambition   b. merit   c. advantage

3. When you feel really awful, you feel _____.
   a. fearsome   b. defiant   c. wretched

4. If you _____ water, you make it clean.
   a. imply   b. purify   c. negotiate

5. To _____ an offer is to take it back.
   a. merit   b. revoke   c. negotiate

6. A(n) _____ is a wish to achieve or to be successful.
   a. ambition   b. advantage   c. merit

7. Something that is _____ can also be described as scary.
   a. fearsome   b. defiant   c. wretched

8. To _____ is to try to reach an agreement.
   a. revoke   b. purify   c. negotiate

9. A job that is well done _____ a reward.
   a. implies   b. merits   c. purifies

10. When you suggest something, you _____ it.
    a. imply   b. merit   c. purify

Synonyms

*Choose the word that is most nearly the **same** in meaning as the word or phrase in **dark print**. Then write your choice on the line provided.*

1. a **disobedient** child
   a. fearsome   b. wretched   c. defiant   _____

2. a daring **aspiration**
   a. ambition   b. advantage   c. merit   _____

3. **discuss** who does the dishes
   a. imply   b. negotiate   c. merit   _____

4. **hint** that they are coming
   a. revoke   b. merit   c. imply   _____

5. **repeal** the offer
   a. purify   b. revoke   c. merit   _____

6. a **virtue** worth rewarding
   a. merit   b. advantage   c. ambition   _____

Antonyms

*Choose the word that is most nearly the **opposite** in meaning to the word or phrase in **dark print**. Then write your choice on the line provided.*

1. an unbelievable **handicap**
   a. advantage   b. ambition   c. merit   _____

2. a **comforting** image
   a. fearsome   b. defiant   c. wretched   _____

3. in **superior** condition
   a. fearsome   b. wretched   c. defiant   _____

4. **contaminate** the air
   a. purify   b. negotiate   c. revoke   _____

Completing the Sentence

From the list of words on pages 112–113, choose the one that best completes each item below. Then write the word on the line provided. (You may have to change the word's ending.)

Baking

Our family has a tradition of baking a cake every Sunday. The _____ to baking on Sunday is that the whole family is home and nobody is rushing off to school or work.

If we misbehave, our baking privileges are _____, and our fun is taken away.

We use only the best ingredients in our cakes, and we _____ the tap water by using a water filter.

I like banana cake, but my parents prefer carrot cake. We have to _____ which cake to make.

The cake comes out great! It always _____ compliments and praise.

I have learned that if we kids _____ that we want a piece of cake, no one will respond. We have to ask for it directly!

Polar Bears

Polar bears are aggressive and powerful hunters and can be quite _____. It is only when people are _____ and confront a bear that they put themselves in danger.

Polar bears live in very cold climates. To us it might seem like a _____ way to live, but polar bears love the cold and ice. Their furry bodies are suited for the cold.

Polar bears are very _____ swimmers. Some bears can swim up to 200 miles at a time in the Arctic Ocean.

Word Associations

*Circle the letter next to the choice that best completes the sentence or answers the question. Pay special attention to the word in **dark print**.*

1. A person who is **defiant** might be
   a. hungry
   b. sleepy
   c. weak
   d. brave

2. Which **implies** that you are sad?
   a. "I'm not in a very jolly mood."
   b. "I feel like I could eat a horse!"
   c. "I am floating on air!"
   d. "I love fried chicken."

3. You must **purify** drinking water if it is
   a. cold.
   b. polluted.
   c. fresh.
   d. wet.

4. After a **wretched** night without sleep,
   a. you feel great.
   b. you feel rested.
   c. you feel tired.
   d. you want dinner.

5. A **fearsome** dog may make you
   a. bark.
   b. growl.
   c. tremble.
   d. laugh.

6. In summer, it's an **advantage** to
   a. have hot soup.
   b. have mittens.
   c. have a snow suit.
   d. have an air conditioner.

7. A movie that has **merit** is likely to
   a. be in black-and-white.
   b. win an award.
   c. come with free popcorn.
   d. have actors in it.

8. If your free pass is **revoked**, you
   a. may enter without paying.
   b. will not be allowed to pay.
   c. will have to pay to enter.
   d. will have to go home.

9. When you **negotiate**, your goal is to
   a. sink or swim.
   b. laugh or cry.
   c. give and take.
   d. dance and sing.

10. Someone with strong **ambition**
    a. tries to be a failure.
    b. tries to be lazy.
    c. tries to be a great success.
    d. doesn't care about anything.

Definitions

Study the spelling, pronunciation, part of speech, and definition for each word. Write the word on the line in the sentence. Then read the synonyms and antonyms.

1. **absorb**
   (əb 'sôrb)

   (v.) to soak up or take in; to keep the attention of

   A sponge can _____ every last drop of water.

   SYNONYMS: consume, devour, assimilate; engage, captivate, engross
   ANTONYMS: discharge, emanate, emit, secrete

2. **amateur**
   ('a mə tər)

   (n.) someone who does something for pleasure and not for money; someone who does not have much experience

   The young actor in the show was an _____.

   SYNONYMS: devotee; beginner, nonprofessional, layman, tyro
   ANTONYMS: expert, professional, master

3. **channel**
   ('cha nəl)

   (n.) the deepest part of a river; a body of water that links two larger ones; a long, narrow groove; a band of radio waves; a course of action

   Many ships passed through the _____.

   (v.) to make a long, narrow groove; to direct or focus

   They began to _____ through the rock.

   SYNONYMS: (n.) passage, strait, waterway, canal; conduit; course, way, direction, path, approach; (v.) plow, cut, furrow; direct, convey, guide

4. **elegant**
   ('e li gənt)

   (adj.) showing beauty, high quality, and good taste

   The diamond is an _____ jewel.

   SYNONYMS: stylish, graceful, exquisite, charming, refined, cultured
   ANTONYMS: coarse, crude, inelegant, unfashionable, rough, gauche

5. **grace**
   (grās)

   (n.) ease and beauty of movement; a charming or pleasing quality; a short prayer at meals

   The horse galloped with incredible _____.

   (v.) to add beauty or honor to

Children raise their voices in song at an **amateur** (word 2) musical production.

Will she _____ our party with her presence?

SYNONYMS: (n.) elegance, gracefulness, loveliness, charm, refinement; blessing; (v.) enhance, enrich, adorn, decorate; honor, favor, glorify
ANTONYMS: (n.) ugliness, inelegance; (v.) disgrace

6. inspect
(in 'spekt)

(v.) to look over closely

Will you please _____ the clothes for any damage?

SYNONYMS: examine, check, investigate, probe, scan

7. lame
(lām)

(adj.) stiff, sore, or not able to move properly; weak, not satisfactory

I cannot swim because of my _____ arm.

SYNONYMS: disabled, limping, sore, inadequate, ineffectual, weak; feeble, flimsy, unconvincing, unsatisfactory; ANTONYMS: strong, healthy; adequate

8. suspend
(sə 'spend)

(v.) to hang in order to allow free movement; to stop for a time, interrupt; to bar from a position or privilege

Please _____ those streamers from the ceiling.

SYNONYMS: hang, dangle; stop, adjourn, interrupt, postpone, delay, halt; remove, exclude; ANTONYMS: continue, resume, prolong

9. tiresome
('tīr səm)

(adj.) annoyingly dull or exhausting; unexciting

Scrubbing the kitchen floor can be _____.

SYNONYMS: boring, annoying, irritating, monotonous, tedious, wearisome
ANTONYMS: interesting, exciting, energizing, stimulating, pleasant

10. tranquil
('trang quəl)

(adj.) free from trouble or disturbance, peaceful and quiet

I enjoyed the _____ day at the lake.

SYNONYMS: calm, peaceful, serene, placid, relaxing, composed
ANTONYMS: noisy, disturbed, excited

Choose the word whose meaning is suggested by the clue given. Then write the word on the line provided.

1. When you stop an activity for a short while, you _____ it.
   a. absorb   b. suspend   c. inspect

2. If you are a(n) _____, you are a beginner.
   a. channel   b. amateur   c. grace

3. An irritating chore can be described as _____.
   a. tiresome   b. tranquil   c. elegant

4. To _____ something is to soak it up.
   a. channel   b. suspend   c. absorb

5. At mealtimes, some families recite _____.
   a. grace   b. amateur   c. channel

6. Something that is _____ is peaceful and serene.
   a. elegant   b. lame   c. tranquil

7. To make a groove is to _____.
   a. channel   b. suspend   c. inspect

8. Someone who is _____ may not be able to move properly.
   a. elegant   b. lame   c. tranquil

9. If you _____ an object, you look at it closely.
   a. absorb   b. grace   c. inspect

10. When something is high-quality, it is _____.
   a. elegant   b. lame   c. tiresome

Synonyms
*Choose the word that is most nearly the **same** in meaning as the word or phrase in **dark print**. Then write your choice on the line provided.*

1. boats through the **canal**
   a. grace   b. amateur   c. channel   _____

2. **scrutinize** my face
   a. inspect   b. absorb   c. suspend   _____

3. a **boring** bike ride
   a. elegant   b. tranquil   c. tiresome   _____

4. an **inadequate** excuse
   a. lame   b. elegant   c. tranquil   _____

5. **consume** my attention
   a. grace   b. absorb   c. inspect   _____

Antonyms
*Choose the word that is most nearly the **opposite** in meaning to the word or phrase in **dark print**. Then write your choice on the line provided.*

1. a **master** at carpentry
   a. channel   b. amateur   c. grace   _____

2. the **coarse** fabric
   a. elegant   b. lame   c. tranquil   _____

3. a **noisy** place
   a. tiresome   b. tranquil   c. lame   _____

4. **prolong** the trip
   a. absorb   b. inspect   c. suspend   _____

5. the monster's **ugliness**
   a. amateur   b. channel   c. grace   _____

From the list of words on pages 118–119, choose the one that best completes each item below. Then write the word on the line provided. (You may have to change the word's ending.)

Presidents

The life of the president of the United States is not a _____ one. It is full of activity and excitement.

Presidents must be hardworking. They have to _____ all their energy into their job.

Some duties of the office are _____. It may be tedious to _____ all the papers that need to be signed, but that's one of the responsibilities of the president!

Franklin Delano Roosevelt, who was president from 1933 to 1945, was made _____ by a disease called polio. He could not walk without braces.

George Washington had to _____ his life as a farmer to become president. He loved his farm in Virginia almost as much as his country.

First Ladies

The wives of American presidents are called first ladies. Jacqueline Kennedy, who was married to John F. Kennedy, was considered _____ because she was beautiful and stylish.

Eleanor Roosevelt became very _____ in her role as first lady and gave it her full attention. Most of the presidents' wives have had experience in politics before they came to the White House. They have not been _____.

It is difficult to say which first lady had the most charm and _____. All of the women have been important to our country.

*Circle the letter next to the choice that best completes the sentence or answers the question. Pay special attention to the word in **dark print**.*

1. Why do most **amateurs** skate?
   a. because it is their job
   b. because they are experts
   c. to get rich
   d. just for the fun of it

2. To **inspect** a bicycle, you can
   a. check its tires and gears.
   b. read a bicycle magazine.
   c. glance at it quickly.
   d. lock it in the garage.

3. A **tiresome** task might make you
   a. burst into song.
   b. feel excited and happy.
   c. repeat it as soon as possible.
   d. complain of boredom.

4. To **suspend** a glass ornament,
   a. take a photo of it.
   b. sell it to a museum.
   c. hang it in your window.
   d. wrap it in soft padding.

5. Which animal runs with **grace**?
   a. a walrus
   b. a camel
   c. a turtle
   d. a deer

6. **Elegant** dinners often include
   a. paper plates and plastic forks.
   b. flowers, candles, and silver.
   c. baby food and bottles.
   d. hot dogs and popcorn.

7. A **lame** research paper is probably
   a. a good one.
   b. a well-done one.
   c. a poor one.
   d. one I would like to hand in.

8. The English **Channel** is
   a. a television program.
   b. a wild party spot.
   c. a body of water.
   d. a city near London.

9. A **tranquil** scene is
   a. calm.
   b. noisy.
   c. busy.
   d. exciting.

10. If a book **absorbs** me, I
    a. put it back on the shelf.
    b. wipe it with a sponge.
    c. can't stop reading it.
    d. write my name in it

Definitions

Study the spelling, pronunciation, part of speech, and definition for each word. Write the word on the line in the sentence. Then read the synonyms and antonyms.

1. boast
(bōst)

(v.) to speak proudly of oneself, brag; to take pride in

The team members tend to _____ whenever they win.

(n.) talk that is too full of pride in oneself

My _____ about my grades drove away my friends.

SYNONYMS: (v.) brag, crow, exaggerate, flaunt, overstate; have, own, enjoy; (n.) pride, self-praise, pretension, swaggering
ANTONYMS: (v.) deprecate, belittle

2. eloquent
('el ə kwənt)

(adj.) showing the ability to use words clearly and effectively

Our minister gave an _____ sermon this morning.

SYNONYMS: expressive, well-spoken, articulate, persuasive, forceful, powerful, effective, charismatic; ANTONYMS: awkward, inarticulate, tongue-tied

3. glisten
('gli sən)

(v.) to shine with sparkling light

I like to see the morning dew _____ in the sunshine.

SYNONYMS: shine, sparkle, glimmer, glitter, shimmer, gleam

4. ideal
(ī 'dēl)

(adj.) considered to be perfect; existing only in the imagination

Today was an _____ spring day.

(n.) a person or thing that is considered to be perfect

My _____ is a world without violence.

SYNONYMS: (adj.) complete, supreme, flawless, exemplary, ultimate; abstract, conceptual; (n.) model, example, epitome, paragon, paradigm
ANTONYMS: (adj.) practical, pragmatic, real, substantial

5. infectious
(in 'fek shəs)

(adj.) caused or spread by germs; able or tending to spread from one to another

Chicken pox is a highly _____ disease.

SYNONYMS: contagious, transmittable, catching, communicable

Martin Luther King, Jr. was an **eloquent** (word 2) speaker who had a very powerful influence on the civil rights movement.

6. invest
(in 'vest)

(v.) to put money into something that will earn interest or make a profit; to make use of for future benefit

They will _____ their money in stocks and bonds.

SYNONYMS: spend, expend, contribute

7. locate
('lō kāt)

(v.) to find the position of; to settle into a place

I need to _____ the highway on the map.

SYNONYMS: find, discover, identify, pinpoint, detect, uncover; settle, situate, build, establish

8. ripple
('ri pəl)

(n.) a light wave

The pebble caused a _____ in the pool.

(v.) to form or cause small waves

A rowboat will _____ the surface of the lake.

SYNONYMS: (n.) wave, vibration; (v.) ruffle, spread, oscillate, undulate

9. sufficient
(sə 'fi shənt)

(adj.) as much as is needed, enough

We have a _____ amount of time to finish our task.

SYNONYMS: enough, adequate, plenty, ample
ANTONYMS: insufficient, inadequate, deficient, lacking, sparse, scanty

10. uproar
('əp rôr)

(n.) a state of noisy excitement, confusion

When I entered, I found the room to be in an _____.

SYNONYMS: turmoil, disorder, confusion, commotion, disturbance, excitement, bedlam, clamor; ANTONYMS: calmness, serenity, tranquillity

 **Match the Meaning**

Choose the word whose meaning is suggested by the clue given. Then write the word on the line provided.

1. If you put money into something that will earn more money, you
   _____ it.
   a. invest   b. ripple   c. boast

2. To brag is also to _____.
   a. glisten   b. boast   c. locate

3. When you find something, you _____ it.
   a. ripple   b. invest   c. locate

4. A well-spoken person can be described as _____.
   a. ideal   b. infectious   c. eloquent

5. A(n) _____ is a small wave.
   a. uproar   b. ripple   c. boast

6. To have a(n) _____ amount is to have as much as you need.
   a. eloquent   b. infectious   c. sufficient

7. A disease that can be caught by others is said to be _____.
   a. infectious   b. sufficient   c. ideal

8. Something that is _____ is considered to be perfect.
   a. eloquent   b. sufficient   c. ideal

9. If you cause a(n) _____, you create much excitement.
   a. uproar   b. boast   c. ripple

10. When an object shines, it might _____.
    a. locate   b. glisten   c. invest

Synonyms

*Choose the word that is most nearly the **same** in meaning as the word or phrase in **dark print.** Then write your choice on the line provided.*

1. a **contagious** laugh
   a. sufficient   b. infectious   c. eloquent   _____

2. created a **wave**
   a. ripple   b. uproar   c. boast   _____

3. **shimmer** under the moonlight
   a. boast   b. glisten   c. locate   _____

4. **find** your gloves
   a. invest   b. glisten   c. locate   _____

5. **expend** my time
   a. boast   b. ripple   c. invest   _____

6. an unnecessary **disturbance**
   a. ripple   b. uproar   c. boast   _____

Antonyms

*Choose the word that is most nearly the **opposite** in meaning to the word or phrase in **dark print.** Then write your choice on the line provided.*

1. **belittle** oneself in front of others
   a. ripple   b. locate   c. boast about   _____

2. a **pragmatic** solution
   a. ideal   b. infectious   c. sufficient   _____

3. a **scanty** amount of food
   a. eloquent   b. infectious   c. sufficient   _____

4. a **fumbling** speech
   a. ideal   b. eloquent   c. infectious   _____

Public Speaking

It is an art to be a good public speaker. The most _____ speakers know how to speak clearly and effectively.

The United States can _____ of many political leaders who were and are excellent communicators.

The moods and emotions of a speaker can be so _____ that those same feelings are felt by the audience.

Sometimes, a speaker chooses to discuss a topic over which there are differences of opinion. At the end of a powerful speech that addresses such a topic, the room might be in an _____.

When audiences enjoy a speaker, a _____ of applause often turns into thunderous applause.

Antoni Gaudí

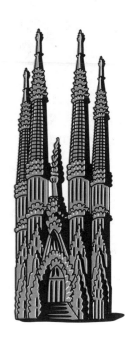

Antoni Gaudí was a Spanish architect. He is known for the original and imaginative designs of his buildings. He found the use of bright colors to be an _____ way to make his buildings stand out.

My favorite Gaudí works are those that look like the scales of a dragon. I especially like looking at them when the sun _____ upon them.

Gaudí's most famous creation is La Sagrada Família, a church _____ in Barcelona.

Gaudí _____ many years in this project, but it is still not finished after more than 100 years! It seems there will never be _____ time to complete it!

Word Associations

*Circle the letter next to the choice that best completes the sentence or answers the question. Pay special attention to the word in **dark print**.*

1. Which makes the eyes **glisten**?
   a. tears
   b. blindfold
   c. tissues
   d. eyebrows

2. **Eloquent** speakers usually
   a. avoid talking in public.
   b. use strong or moving words.
   c. sound awkward or nervous.
   d. forget the right words.

3. When you **locate** your assigned seat, you
   a. have to ask an usher to seat you.
   b. have lost your way.
   c. have found the right one.
   d. have left the theater.

4. When wheat **ripples**, it
   a. is ready to eat.
   b. stands still.
   c. tears and breaks.
   d. moves in gentle waves.

5. My **ideal** home would be
   a. too small.
   b. filled with mosquitos.
   c. perfect in every way.
   d. a nightmare to care for.

6. Which is a **boast**?
   a. "I like your new haircut."
   b. "I am the best artist in school."
   c. "I hope I make the team."
   d. "I would be glad to help."

7. People **invest** money to
   a. make even more money.
   b. lose it as fast as they can.
   c. keep it under their mattress.
   d. spend all their money on lottery tickets.

8. During an **uproar**, expect lots of
   a. yawning and snoring.
   b. confusion and noise.
   c. apples and oranges.
   d. peace and quiet.

9. When I hear an **infectious** giggle,
   a. I might ignore it.
   b. I might start to cry.
   c. I might laugh too.
   d. I might call the police.

10. Which might be **sufficient** time to finish a big job?
    a. a day
    b. a minute
    c. a second
    d. no time at all

*Circle the choice that is most nearly the **same** in meaning as the word in **dark print**.*

1. deserves **merit**
   a. praise   b. lunch   c. failure   d. punishment

2. went to a **formal** dance
   a. casual   b. country   c. fancy   d. school

3. could **conceive** such a plan
   a. cancel   b. formulate   c. ruin   d. repeat

4. a **privilege** to meet you
   a. joke   b. mistake   c. rush   d. honor

5. that **tiresome** old game
   a. thrilling   b. challenging   c. childish   d. unexciting

6. **amateur** radio operator
   a. nonprofessional b. master   c. rude   d. silly

7. in **sufficient** quantities
   a. skimpy   b. huge   c. ample   d. spicy

8. to **glisten** with sweat
   a. soak   b. shine   c. drip   d. sleep

9. **penalize** them for cheating
   a. thank   b. punish   c. admire   d. tease

10. in **elegant** velvet robes
    a. rugged   b. bright   c. graceful   d. short

Spelling

*Study the word in **dark print**. If a letter is missing, fill in the blank to make a correctly spelled word. If the word is already spelled correctly, leave the blank empty.*

1. **rev__ke** your rights

2. by the **barr__er**

3. **nego__iate** the deal

4. sweet **s__umber**

5. switch the **ch__nnel**

6. went **la__me**

7. **infe__tious** virus

8. in an **upro__r**

9. **lo__ate** the book

10. was my **ambi__tion**

Antonyms

*Circle the choice that is most nearly the **opposite** in meaning to the word in **dark print**.*

1. to **purify** the mixture
   a. dirty   b. clean   c. stir   d. measure

2. know when to **inquire**
   a. reply   b. ask   c. leave   d. begin

3. near her **picturesque** cottage
   a. tiny   b. charming   c. colorful   d. drab

4. wanted to **suspend** the party
   a. attend   b. cancel   c. prolong   d. organize

5. gave **eloquent** speeches
   a. stirring   b. awkward   c. long   d. serious

Vocabulary in Context

Words have been left out of the following passage. For each numbered item in the passage, fill in the circle next to the word in the margin that best fills the blank space.

Do we get any __1__ from television? Does television make us smarter? Does it open our minds? Or does it keep us from doing more important things? People have been arguing over this ever since TV began. That wasn't so long ago at all.

Scientists began to work on television in the 1800s. Television first went into a few homes in 1928 in New York State. A local station called WGY sent test signals to those homes. The new invention was far from __2__. The first televisions were not nearly as advanced as the ones we have today, but people really liked the new invention. They liked to be able to see shows in their own homes. Groups would gather to watch whatever was on. But there wasn't much to see back then.

There were other __3__ to the rise of early TV. For one thing, TV sets cost a lot of money. Those first sets were so small! They only had 3-inch screens! These tiny screens showed poor, shaky pictures, and only in black and white.

But people were getting hooked. In 1946, the TV boom really took off. Many families saved up to buy TV sets. They loved to __4__ about being the first one on the block to have one. Today, 98 out of every 100 homes have at least one TV set. Many have more than one set. Unlike the old TVs, almost all are color sets now. Even the smallest ones have clear, bright pictures.

Most Americans love television. They cannot imagine life without it. Others worry that we get lazy by __5__ surfing. They say that we could be reading or playing music. Or they say that we could be doing sports, making things, or spending time with friends and family. What do you think?

1. ○ advertising
   ○ advantage
   ○ loss
   ○ ideas

2. ○ ideal
   ○ defiant
   ○ tiresome
   ○ tranquil

3. ○ merits
   ○ partners
   ○ losers
   ○ barriers

4. ○ complain
   ○ invest
   ○ boast
   ○ repeat

5. ○ body
   ○ channel
   ○ speed
   ○ Web

Analogies *Circle the item that best completes the comparison. Then explain the relationship on the lines provided.*

1. **sleepy** is to **slumber** as
   a. tired is to waken
   b. angry is to smile
   c. hungry is to eat
   d. alert is to rest

Relationship: _____

_____

_____

_____

•

3. **amateur** is to **expert** as
   a. abundant is to meager
   b. teacher is to artist
   c. writer is to poet
   d. soldier is to farmer

Relationship: _____

_____

_____

_____

2. **lame** is to **walk** as
   a. blind is to taste
   b. hand is to foot
   c. blame is to see
   d. deaf is to hear

Relationship: _____

_____

_____

4. **sponge** is to **absorb** as
   a. bucket is to water
   b. broom is to sweep
   c. dust is to mop
   d. washer is to dryer

Relationship: _____

_____

_____

Challenge: Make up your own
Write a comparison using the words in the box. Then write the relationship on the lines provided.

sufficient	tranquil	peaceful	enough

Analogy: _____ is to _____ as _____ is to _____ .

Relationship: _____

_____

Word Families

*The words in **dark print** in the sentences below are related to words introduced in Units 13–16. For example, the nouns* infection *and* tranquility *in Item 1 are related to the adjectives* tranquil *(Unit 15) and* infectious *(Unit 16). Based on your understanding of the unit words, circle the related word in **dark print** that best completes each sentence.*

absorb	defiance	grace	inspect	predator
advantage	elegant	ideal	invest	privilege
ambition	formal	infectious	locate	suspend
boast	glisten	inquire	negotiate	tranquil

1. So much **(infection/tranquility)** is rare in a busy city.

2. A police **(investor/negotiator)** got the hijacker to give up.

3. Fluffy, thick towels are usually very **(absorbent/glistening)**.

4. Radar and sonar help us find the **(inspection/location)** of sunken ships.

5. If you don't give me time to do my work, you will put me at a **(disadvantage/formality)**.

6. Putting on a play is our most **(ambitious/predatory)** project so far.

7. We were impressed by the **(elegance/suspension)** of the costumes.

8. Ballet is a **(boastful/graceful)** form of dancing.

9. Don't **(idealize/defy)** the past; life was hard then, too.

10. **(Inquiring/Privileged)** minds always want to know more.

Use the clue and the given letters to complete each word. Write the missing letters of the word in the appropriate boxes. Then use the circled letters and the drawing to answer the CHALLENGE question below.

1. to suggest something without saying it directly

☐ M (☐) ☐ Y

2. unhappy or unfortunate

W ☐ (☐) ☐ C H ☐ (☐)

3. frightening or alarming

☐ ☐ A (☐) S (☐) M ☐

4. to look over closely

☐ N ☐ ☐ E ☐ (☐)

5. a small wave

(☐) I ☐ ☐ L E

6. a state of noisy excitement

☐ ☐ R ☐ (☐) ☐

Challenge:

What can you call this kind of creature?

☐ ☐ ☐ ☐ ☐ ☐ ☐ ☐

Definitions *Choose the word from the box that matches each definition. Write the word on the line provided. The first one has been done for you.*

admirable	~~meek~~	revoke
audible	modest	scorn
barrier	negotiate	valid
infectious	origin	watchful
lame	picturesque	woe

1. not courageous or strong   meek

2. always noticing what is happening, aware

3. great sorrow or suffering; trouble

4. not boastful; proper in speech, dress, or behavior

5. deserving praise

6. to discuss in order to arrive at an agreement

7. to cancel by withdrawing or reversing

8. charming, quaint, suitable for a picture

9. stiff or sore; weak, not satisfactory

10. caused or spread by germs

 **Antonyms** *Choose the word from the box that is most nearly **opposite** in meaning to each group of words. Write the word on the line provided. The first one has been done for you.*

1. deny, invalidate   <u>declare</u>

2. disgrace, dishonor, shame   _____

3. allow, permit   _____

4. cowardly, timid; infirm, weak, thin   _____

5. bewilder, complicate, mystify, puzzle   _____

6. ordinary, plain, simple   _____

7. cheery, lively, merry   _____

8. drawback, handicap   _____

9. casual, informal, unofficial   _____

10. deficient, scarce, meager   _____

11. discharge, emit, secrete, emanate   _____

12. deficient, inadequate, lacking, scanty   _____

13. reject, condemn, discredit   _____

14. near, close, adjacent   _____

15. end, finish   _____

absorb
abundant
advantage
approve
clarify
~~declare~~
distant
dreary
formal
glory
magnificent
origin
prevent
stout
sufficient

Completing the Sentence

Choose the word from the box that best completes each sentence below. Write the word on the line provided. The first one has been done for you.

Group A

| approach | consume | ~~devotion~~ |
| grave | punctuate | yearn |

1. The players show total _____devotion_____ to their team.

2. We knew by the _____ look on all of their faces that something was terribly wrong.

3. Do you know how to _____ dialogue in a story?

4. It is always wise to _____ a strange dog slowly and carefully.

Group B

| ambition | glisten | grace |
| inquire | locate | wretched |

1. This _____ mess is too much for one person to clean up.

2. Where do I _____ about joining this health club?

3. She had the good _____ to bring flowers to her host.

4. We plan to _____ a vacation spot that is perfect for our family and friends.

 **Classifying**

Choose the word from the box that goes best with each group of words. Write the word on the line provided. Then explain what the words have in common. The first one has been done for you.

arch	boast	fearsome	invest
purify	~~representative~~	revive	slumber

1. president, senator, governor, _____representative_____

   The words name public leaders whom people vote for.

2. wall, roof, window, _____

   _____

3. pure, purity, _____, impure

   _____

4. snooze, nap, doze, _____

   _____

5. adventuresome, awesome, _____, tiresome

   _____

6. save, spend, donate, _____

   _____

7. host, toast, most, _____

   _____

8. refresh, repeat, replace, _____

   _____

FINAL MASTERY TEST

Definitions *Choose the word that matches the definition. Then write the word on the line provided.*

1. to hook something up; to hold onto tightly
   a. clasp   b. gasp   c. glance   d. intend   _____

2. to uncover or open to view; to make something known
   a. explore   b. expose   c. boast   d. absorb   _____

3. a feeling that something or someone is worthless or inferior
   a. arch   b. ideal   c. stunt   d. scorn   _____

4. one that catches or devours others; an animal that stalks and eats other animals
   a. journey   b. resource   c. predator   d. merit   _____

5. to suggest something without saying it directly
   a. revive   b. conceive   c. glisten   d. imply   _____

6. someone who does something for pleasure and not for money
   a. bargain   b. amateur   c. treasure   d. triumph   _____

7. to take part in a game or contest; to play against another or others
   a. compete   b. accuse   c. consider   d. conquer   _____

8. strong anger, rage
   a. fury   b. wit   c. devotion   d. privilege   _____

9. showing an ability to use words clearly and effectively
   a. loyal   b. restless   c. eloquent   d. fierce   _____

10. to try hard; to make a great effort; to fight
    a. disturb   b. plunge   c. exclaim   d. struggle   _____

11. being the real thing; worthy of belief, true
    a. modest   b. admirable c. authentic   d. fearsome   _____

12. measuring little from bottom to top; not deep; not showing much thought
    a. brilliant   b. shallow   c. harsh   d. rare   _____

Part of Speech *Indicate the part of speech of the word in **dark print**. In the space provided, write N for noun, V for verb, or A for adjective.*

13. ____ an **active** puppy

14. ____ a long, winding **passage**

15. ____ **convince** the voters

16. ____ **depart** before dawn

17. ____ along the sandy **coast**

18. ____ **cling** to a life raft

19. ____ a **delightful** smile

20. ____ to the **vibrant** music

21. ____ will **approve** the budget

22. ____ a tough **opponent**

 **Completing the Sentence** *Choose the word from the box that best completes each sentence. Write the word on the line provided. (You may have to change the word's ending.)*

Group A

ambition	audible	barrier	consume
declare	exhaust	glide	merit

23. Some sounds that are not _____ to humans can be heard by animals.

24. At noon, the principal will _____ the name of the winner.

25. Open the door so that the _____ from the motor won't collect inside the garage.

26. It's always been my _____ to climb to the top of Mount Everest.

Group B

climate	honor	observe	penalize
predict	prompt	suspend	uproar

27. The judges may _____ you if you break any of the contest rules.

28. Each year, my neighbors _____ a flag from their window on the Fourth of July.

29. The children made such a(n) _____ that their parents rushed in to see what was wrong.

30. My piano teacher expects me to be _____ for my weekly lesson.

*Circle the letter next to the word or expression that best completes the sentence or answers the question. Pay special attention to the word in **dark print**.*

31. To **vary** the music, you would
    a. always play folk songs.
    b. play different kinds of songs.
    c. shut off the radio.
    d. never sing the words.

32. A person in a **gloomy** mood might
    a. giggle and laugh.
    b. dance around the house.
    c. clown around and juggle.
    d. frown and whine.

33. Which is a **symbol** of love?
    a. a heart
    b. a zebra
    c. a drum
    d. a toaster

34. To **avoid** the party, you might say,
    a. "Oh boy, I can't wait until then!"
    b. "Please, will you invite me?"
    c. "Thanks, but I have other plans."
    d. "What time shall I arrive?"

35. Where do you usually see **wreckage**?
    a. in a junk yard
    b. in a dance studio
    c. in a dressing room
    d. in a jewelry store

36. **Automatic** heaters
    a. need to be turned on and off.
    b. never work right.
    c. work by hand.
    d. go on and off by themselves.

37. If I **inspect** your room, I will
    a. lock the doors and windows.
    b. move all the furniture.
    c. look it over very carefully.
    d. invite you to sleep over.

38. Which is **infectious**?
    a. a splinter
    b. the mumps
    c. your skin
    d. a broken arm

39. To **unite** family members,
    a. get a moving van.
    b. make them have a fight.
    c. bring them all together.
    d. give away all their pets.

40. If you feel a **chill**, you might
    a. turn down the heat.
    b. turn up the volume.
    c. put on the air conditioner.
    d. put on a sweater.

INDEX

The following is a list of all the words taught in the units of this book. The number after each entry indicates the page on which the word is first introduced. The word also appears in exercises on later pages.